The OUTCOME Primers Series 2.0

The MAPPING Primer

Other Books in This Series

The OUTCOME Primer:
Envisioning Learning Outcomes

The ASSESSMENT Primer:
Assessing and Tracking Evidence of Learning Outcomes

The CONTENT Primer:
Aligning Essential Content with Learning Outcomes

The GUIDING Primer:
Guiding Toward Learning Outcomes

The SUSTAINABILITY Primer:
Sustaining Learning Outcomes and Assessment

THE MAPPING PRIMER
MAPPING THE WAY TO LEARNING OUTCOMES

Ruth Stiehl
Founder, The Learning Organization
Professor Emeritus, Instructional Systems
Oregon State University

Kathy Telban
President, Chief Outcome Strategist and Coach, iSOLVit LLC
Past Board Member, White Water Institute for Leadership Training
Former Director of Curriculum Development and Learning Outcome Assessment,
Cuyahoga Community College

The Learning Organization

The MAPPING Primer:
Mapping the Way to Learning Outcomes

Ruth Stiehl and Kathy Telban

Print Edition Copyright © 2017
The Learning Organization
Corvallis, Oregon
Library of Congress Control Number: 2016902288
ISBN: 978-1523634026

Executive Editor: Don Prickel
Assistant Editor: Lori Sours
Editor/Production: Robin McBride
Graphics and Illustrations: Geoffrey Floyd and Robin McBride

CreateSpace Independent Publishing Platform, North Charleston, SC

For further information, visit our website at *www.outcomeprimers.com*
or email us at *strategists@outcomeprimers.com*.

To our families

—RS, KT

Table of Contents

PART TWO: *Using Organic Patterns for Curricular Mapping*

As people pursue any shared enterprise over time, they develop a common practice, that is, shared ways of doing things and relating to one another that allow them to achieve their joint purpose.
　　　　　　　　　　　　　　—Fritjof Capra in *The Hidden Connections*

PART THREE: *Preparing Yourself to Create Curricular Maps*

A map does not just chart, it unlocks and formulates meaning; it forms bridges between here and there, between disparate ideas that we did not know were previously connected.

　　　　　　　　　　　　　—Reif Larsen, *The Collected Works of T. S. Spivet*

PART FOUR: *Mapping Programs: A Facilitator's Guide*

Coming together is the beginning; keeping together is progress; working together is success.

—Henry Ford

PART FIVE: *Bringing It All Together in a Four-Page Curriculum Plan*

We can hire instructors for their expertise in subject matter, but it is our responsibility to show them how their work (course) is connected to the larger picture of learner success.

The Purpose of This Book Stated as a Learning Outcome

Working through this book should help build your capacity to:

- Create a visual map of the learner's journey through a series of learning experiences in programs and courses.
- Facilitate mapping sessions to align outcomes, improve sequencing, and use resources to achieve intended learning outcomes.

The OUTCOME Primers Series 2.0

The OUTCOME Primer: *Envisioning Learning Outcomes*

What do learners need to be able to do in real-life roles that we are responsible for in programs, courses, and workshops?

The ASSESSMENT Primer: *Assessing and Tracking Evidence of Learning Outcomes*

What can learners do to show evidence of the intended outcomes and how will the evidence be documented, tracked, and used?

The CONTENT Primer: *Aligning Essential Content with Learning Outcomes*

What concepts, skills, and issues are essential for learners to achieve the intended outcomes?

The MAPPING Primer: *Mapping the Way to Learning Outcomes*

How do we assure that the learner's journey aligns with the intended outcomes?

The GUIDING Primer: *Guiding Toward Learning Outcomes*

What do effective *guides* do that is so different from our traditional notion of *teaching*?

The SUSTAINABILITY Primer: *Sustaining Learning Outcomes and Assessment*

How do we create a system of learning outcomes and assessment so the work is sustained?

Once a Fad—Now a Fact!

When we published the very first OUTCOMES Primer in the year 2000, academic and workplace training programs were deemed a success based on seat time, bodies in the seats, and the number of topics covered; the transfer of learning to real-life roles was little more than an afterthought.

It has taken the past fifteen years for professional organizations and accreditation agencies to move the adult education industry into adopting an outcome-based framework for curricular planning.

The six Essential Questions addressed in The OUTCOME Primers Series 2.0

- *What do learners need to be able to do in real-life roles that we are responsible for in programs, courses, and workshops?*

- *What can learners do to show evidence of the intended outcomes and how will the evidence be documented, tracked, and used?*

- *What concepts, skills, and issues are essential for the learners to achieve the intended outcomes?*

- *How do we assure that the learner's journey aligns with the intended outcomes?*

- *What do effective* guides *do that is so different from our traditional notion of "teaching"?*

- *How do we create a system of learning outcomes and assessment so the work is sustained?*

Once a fad, now a fact, implementing curricula that are driven by clear and robust learning outcomes is a major challenge for all education programs in universities, community, and technical colleges, as well as the workplace.

It is one thing for an organization to *own* the idea of learning outcomes, and quite another for it to create a sustainable system that includes six key actions: envisioning learning outcomes, aligning essential content with learning outcomes, assessing and tracking evidence of outcomes, mapping learning experiences, guiding learners toward the outcomes, and sustaining the process during other kinds of organizational change. Our newly released *OUTCOME Primers Series 2.0* is designed and structured to make every leader, instructor, and trainer proficient in these six areas of outcomes planning and assessment.

Distinguishing Our Work

If there were two primary things that distinguish our work with outcomes and assessment from all others, it would have to be the understanding of *outside-in* and *the learner's journey.*

In all six Primers, we have sought to apply systems thinking through the concept of *outside-in*—the simple notion that every learning experience is for a purpose outside the learning environment, meaning, in real-life contexts. Planning for a learning experience begins *outside.*

The second thing that distinguishes our work in the Primers is the concept of *the learner's journey.* If there is any unifying visual organizer that can clarify outcome-based learning and assessment in academic and workplace organizations, it is a paddler on a rapidly flowing whitewater river. To us, there is nothing more foundational to outcomes thinking than to carry a mental image of learners on their journey in an ever-changing river of life experiences. In *The GUIDING Primer: Guiding Toward Learning Outcomes,* we reinforce this image by picturing a paddle raft of learners on a whitewater river with the guide at the back, where every rapid is an opportunity to assess learning.

When we envision a workshop, training, course, or program as a sequence of learning experiences that flow from the first class session, *the put-in,* to the last class session, *the take-out,* there seems to be greater clarity about what it means to teach, train, or GUIDE (our preferred word) toward significant outcomes. It is this image of the *learner's journey* and *outside-in* that we carry throughout all the six Primers in this series, and capture, in its simplest form, on the following pages. These two primary distinguishing characteristics of the Primers are illustrated in the overleaf on pages xvi and xvii.

While our approach to understanding outcomes and assessment has not changed from our first primer in 2000, it is quite a departure for us to break outcomes planning into six distinct Primers (a *six-pac*). There are three specific reasons we have selected this small format for our new Series:

- Each Primer highlights one important element in outcome-based planning and can be used independently for intensive professional development.
- We can produce quantities of individual primers inexpensively, meaning organizations can afford to get them in the hands of every trainer and every instructor, not just the leaders.
- Each Primer or the entire series of six books (a *six-pac*) can be printed and shipped literally overnight.

As always, there are trade-offs in keeping the purchase price low and separating the tasks. We have chosen to forego our desire to use color, high-end paper, and fold-out pages. We also take a risk in separating each element of outcomes and assessment from the *whole*; all systems are greater than the individual parts taken separately. The answer is to invest in the *whole*.

It is our hope that these books will prove as useful as the original series we began more than 15 years ago.

—Ruth Stiehl
Corvallis, Oregon
2017

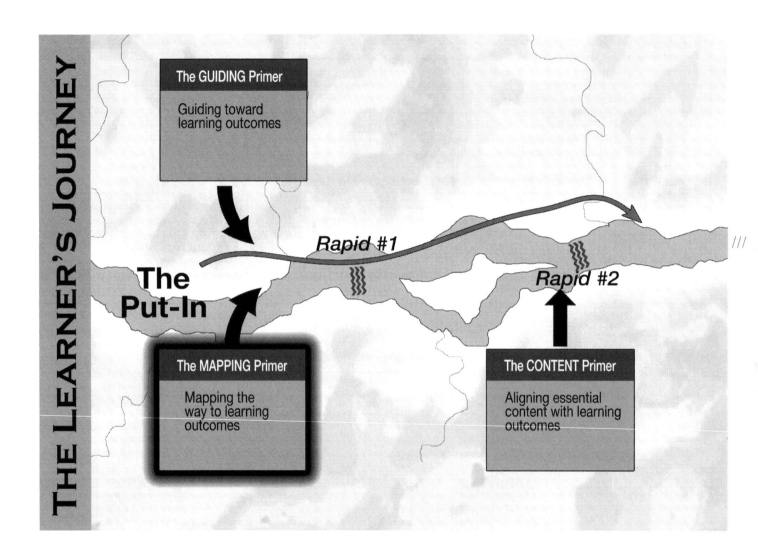

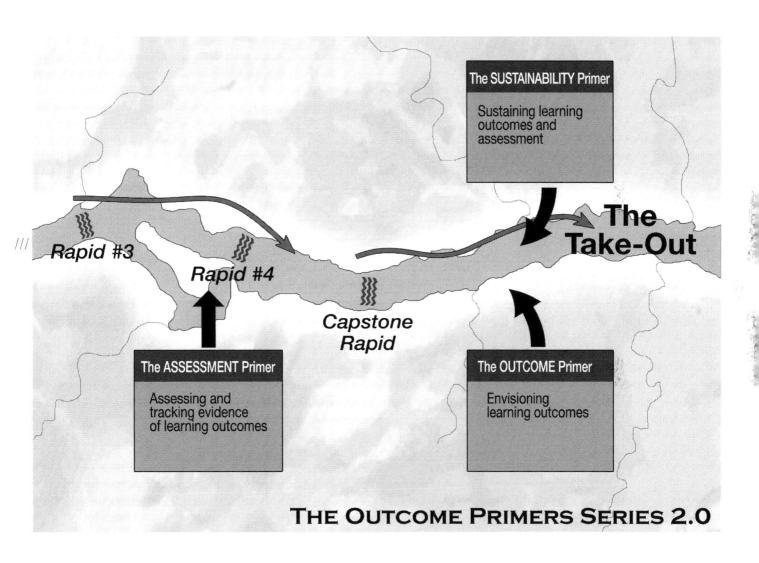

PART ONE

The Power of Visualizing the Way to Learning Outcomes

*Being able to think in visual images reveals connections
and relationships that are difficult to communicate through text.*

Introduction

If a picture is worth a thousand words, a map is worth a thousand pictures.

The unique contribution this Primer makes to outcomes planning is the attention it brings to using visual tools. For that reason, we have chosen not to write an introduction, but rather, to build the introduction through a progression of visual images you can explore. Don't be surprised if you have a lot of questions as you view these images, for that is our intent.

is for SOCIETY

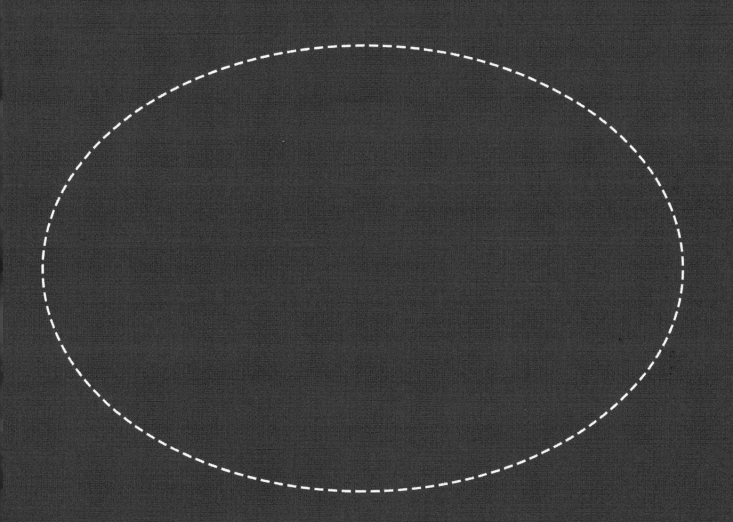

is for an ORGANIZATION

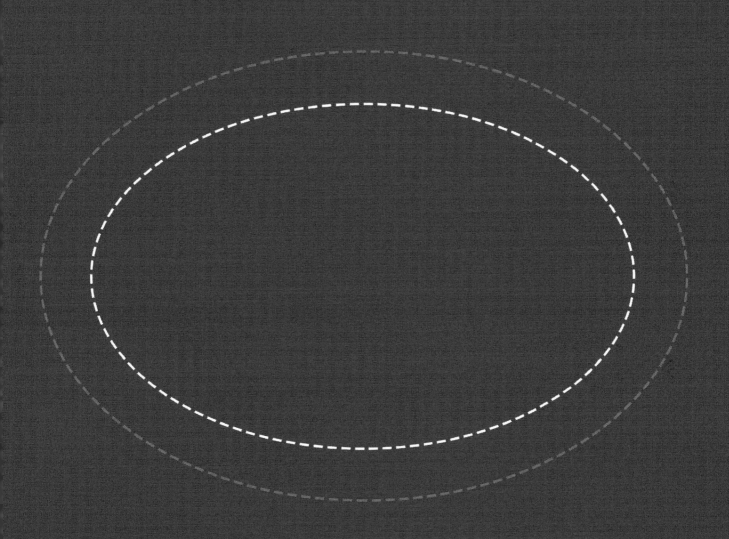

is for training or academic PROGRAM

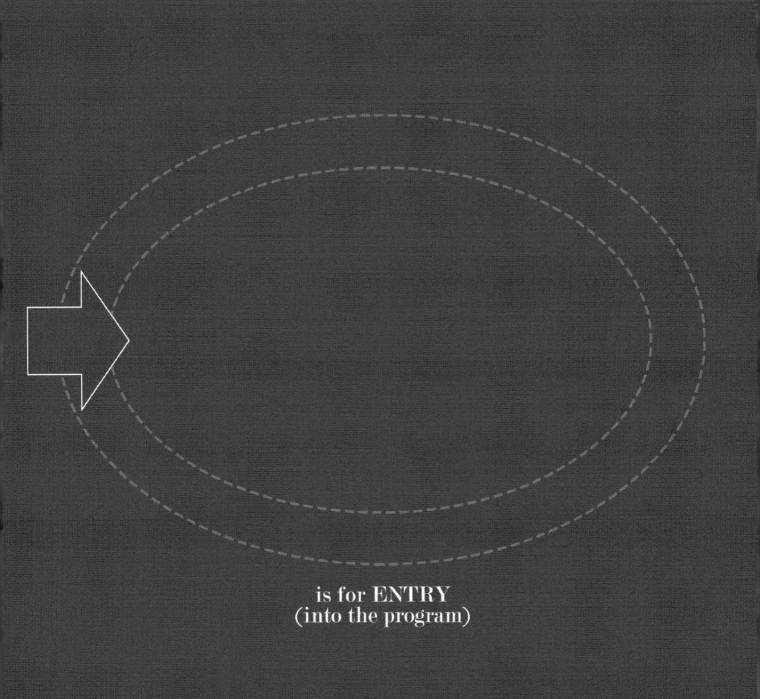

is for ENTRY
(into the program)

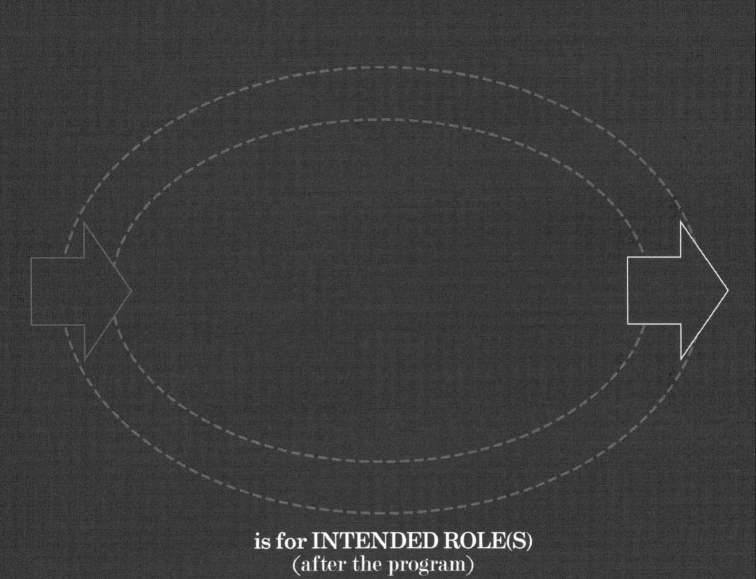

is for INTENDED ROLE(S)
(after the program)

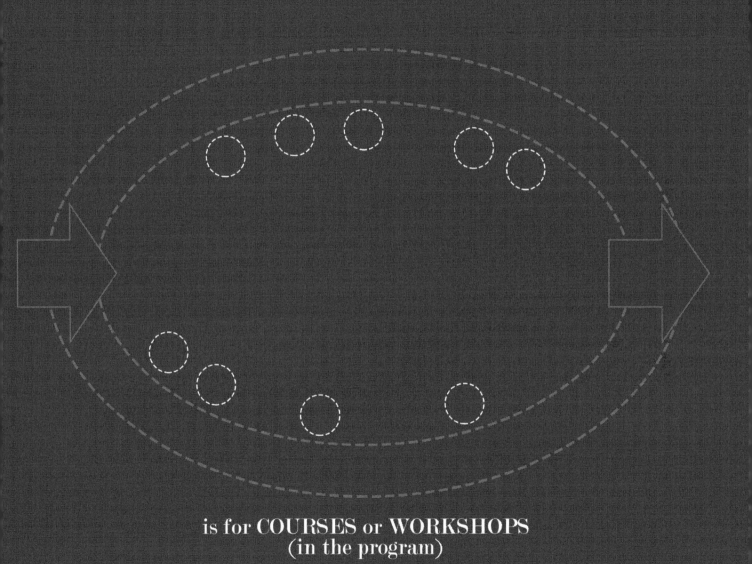

is for COURSES or WORKSHOPS
(in the program)

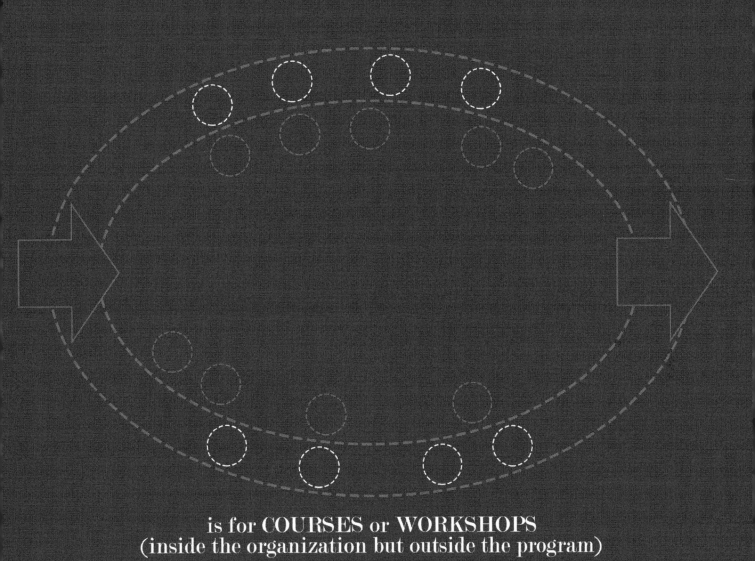

is for COURSES or WORKSHOPS
(inside the organization but outside the program)

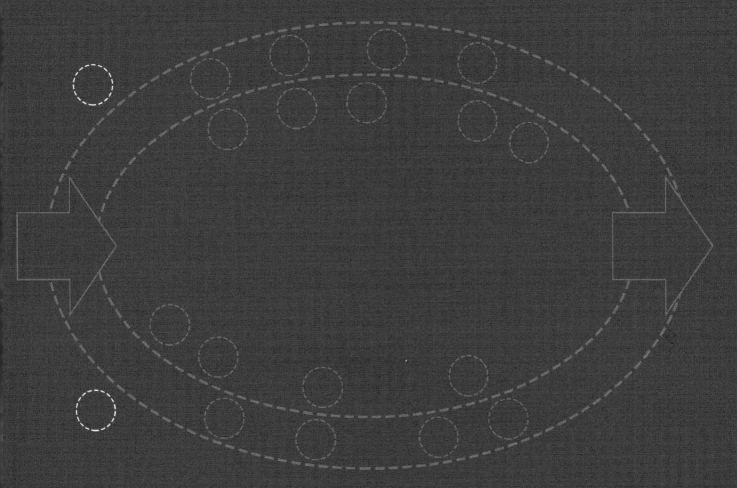

is for LEARNING EXPERIENCES
(outside the organization)

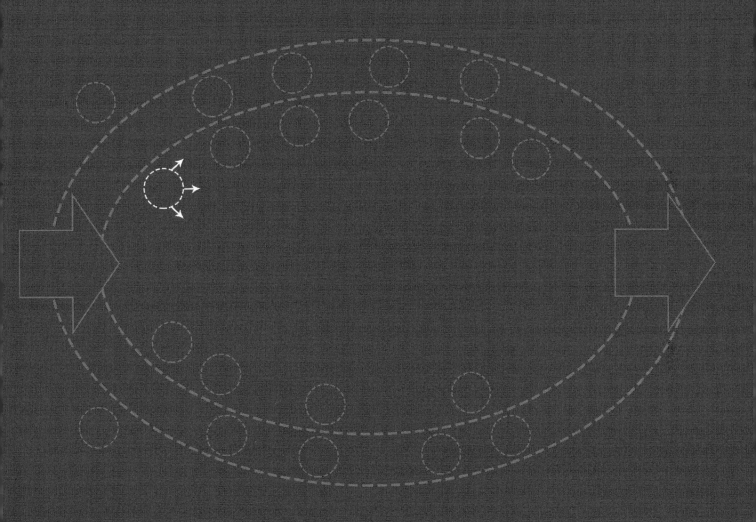

is for INTRODUCTORY COURSE or WORKSHOP

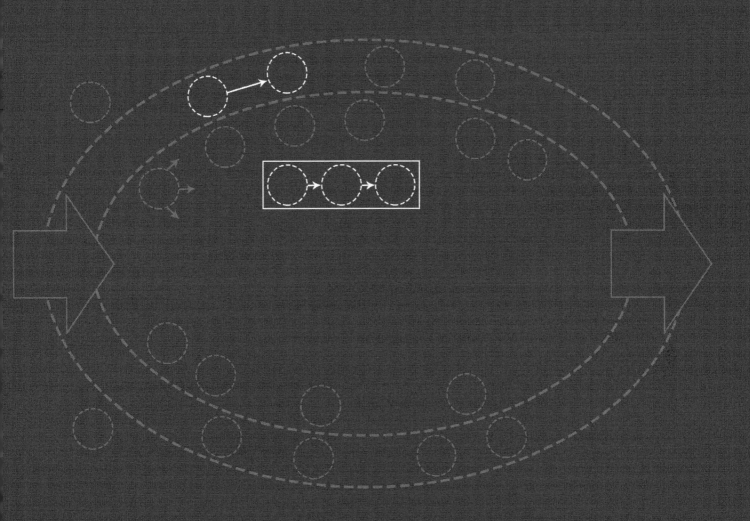

is for COURSE or WORKSHOP SEQUENCE

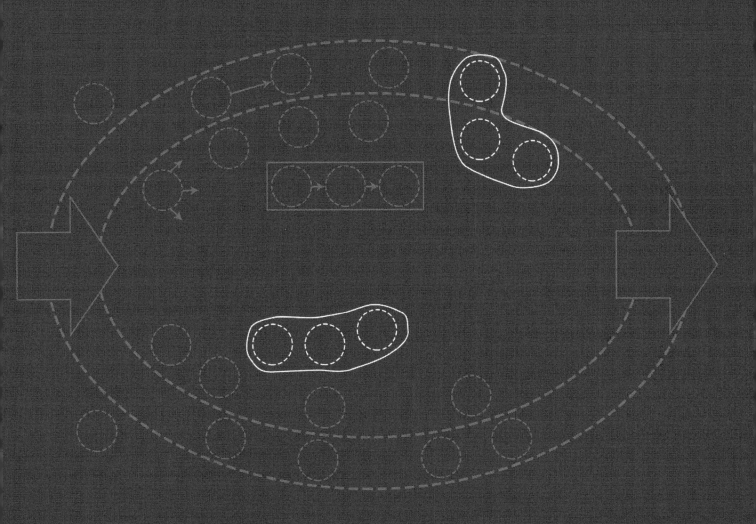

is for THEME CLUSTER

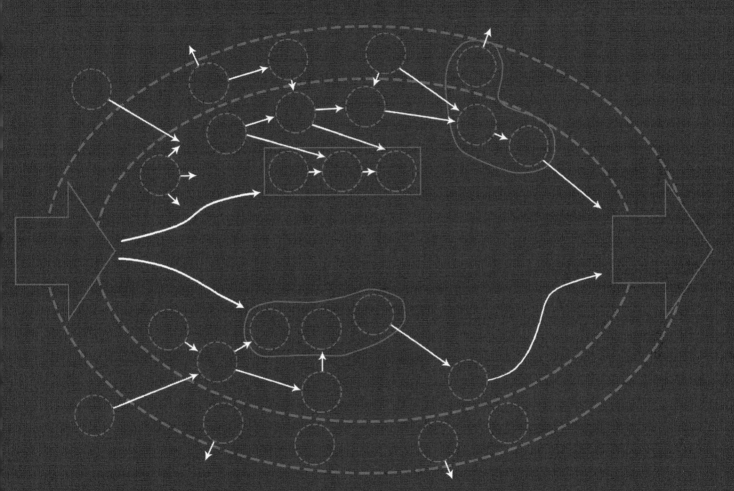

is for CONNECTIONS
(between learning experiences)

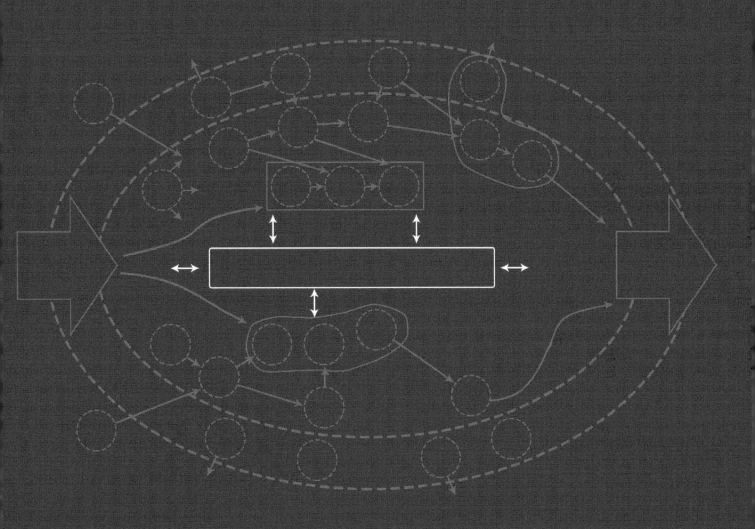

is for an INTEGRATING EXPERIENCE

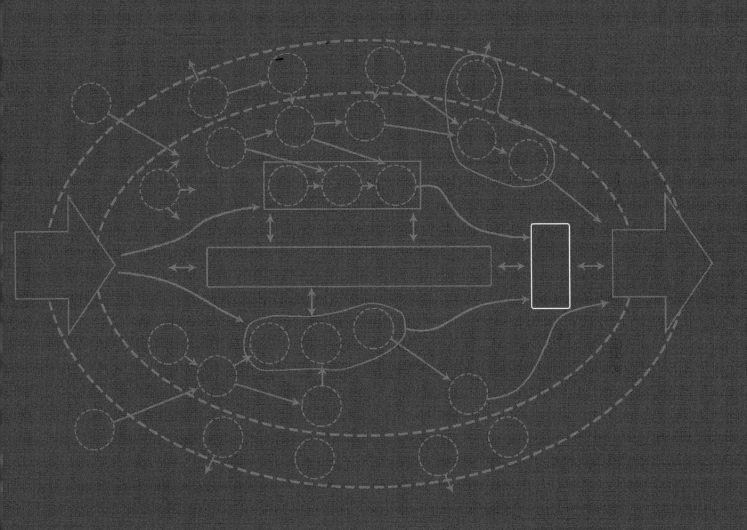

is for CAPSTONE ASSESSMENT

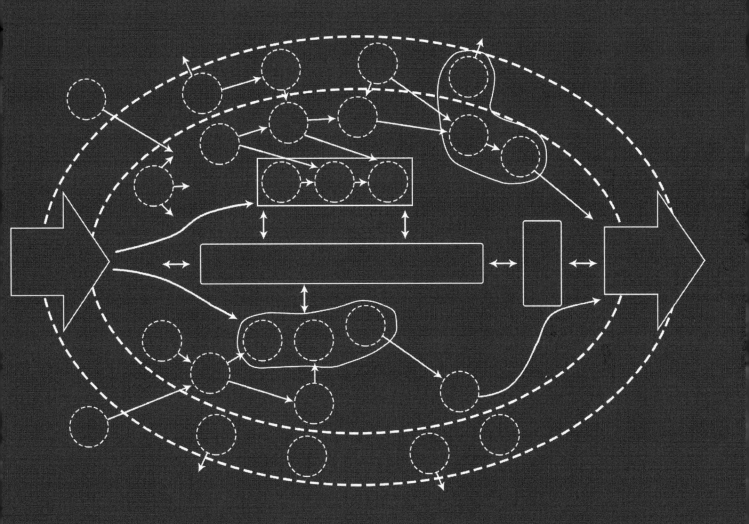

is for PROGRAM MAP

Construction and Forestry Equipment Technology Program Map

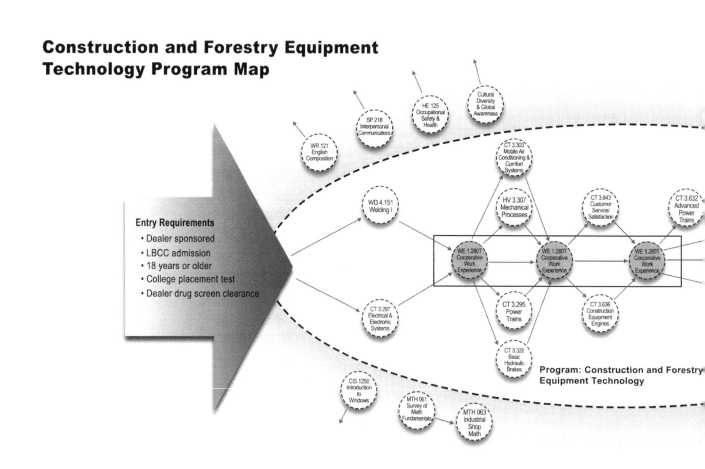

Figure 1: Construction and Forestry Equipment Technology Program Map (Associate Degree)

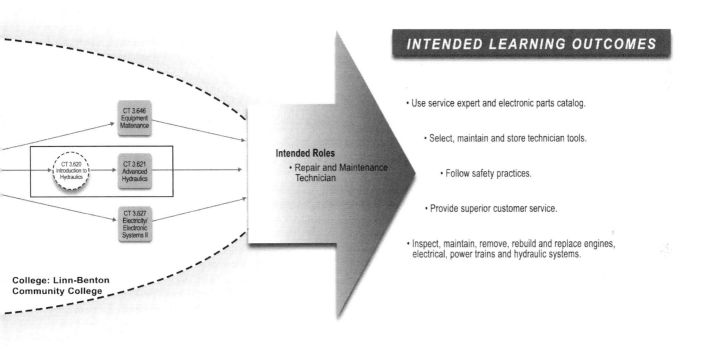

INTENDED LEARNING OUTCOMES

Intended Roles
• Repair and Maintenance Technician

• Use service expert and electronic parts catalog.

• Select, maintain and store technician tools.

• Follow safety practices.

• Provide superior customer service.

• Inspect, maintain, remove, rebuild and replace engines, electrical, power trains and hydraulic systems.

CT 3.646
Equipment
Maintenance

CT 3.620
Introduction to
Hydraulics

CT 3.621
Advanced
Hydraulics

CT 3.627
Electricity/
Electronic
Systems II

College: Linn-Benton Community College

Executive Leadership Program Map

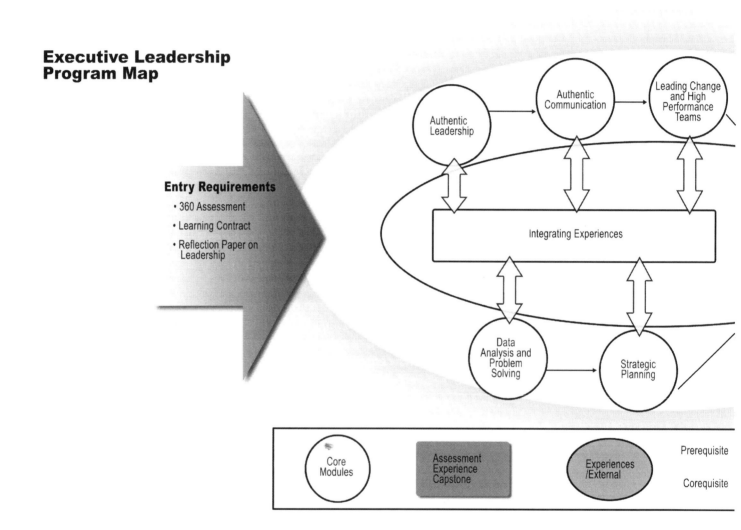

Entry Requirements
- 360 Assessment
- Learning Contract
- Reflection Paper on Leadership

Figure 2: Executive Leadership Program Map (Corporate Training)

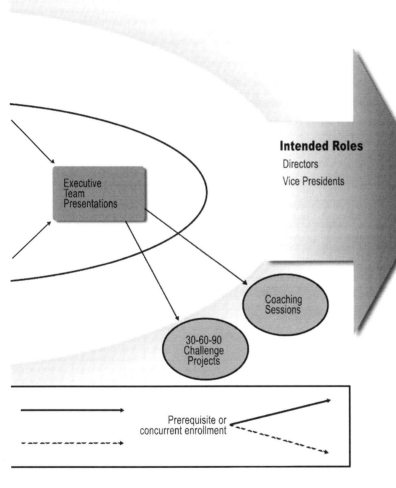

INTENDED LEARNING OUTCOMES

Intended Roles
Directors
Vice Presidents

- Applies authentic leadership and strategies to lead a change initative and to build and lead a diverse high performance team to meet the goals of the organization.

  - Authentically communicates with all stakeholders that will build trust and engage them in organizational initiatives.

    - Networks and builds relationships across the organization by finding common ground and collaborating to solve organizational problems and issues.

    - Integrates and assimilates large complex information to identify and evaluate strategies and solutions during changing conditions.

- Determines strategies, aligns organizational priorities and human capital needs in order to execute, measure and meet organizational outcomes.

Executive Team Presentations

Coaching Sessions

30-60-90 Challenge Projects

Prerequisite or concurrent enrollment

Real Estate Sales / Brokers License Program Map

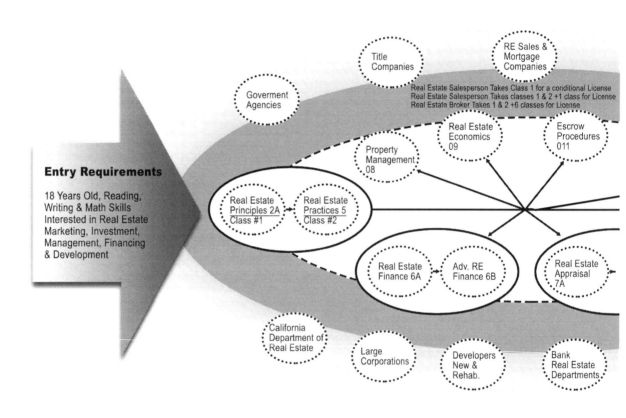

Figure 3: Real Estate Sales/Brokers License Program Map (Professional Development)

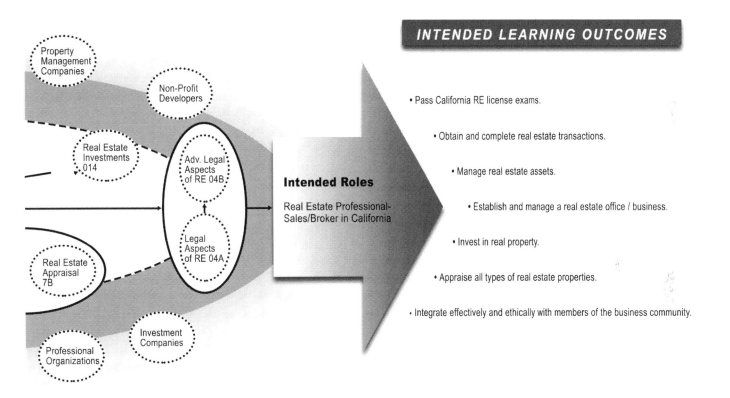

INTENDED LEARNING OUTCOMES

- Pass California RE license exams.

  - Obtain and complete real estate transactions.

    - Manage real estate assets.

      - Establish and manage a real estate office / business.

    - Invest in real property.

  - Appraise all types of real estate properties.

- Integrate effectively and ethically with members of the business community.

Intended Roles

Real Estate Professional-
Sales/Broker in California

Property Management Companies

Non-Profit Developers

Real Estate Investments 014

Adv. Legal Aspects of RE 04B

Legal Aspects of RE 04A

Real Estate Appraisal 7B

Professional Organizations

Investment Companies

Alternative Energy Degree Program Map

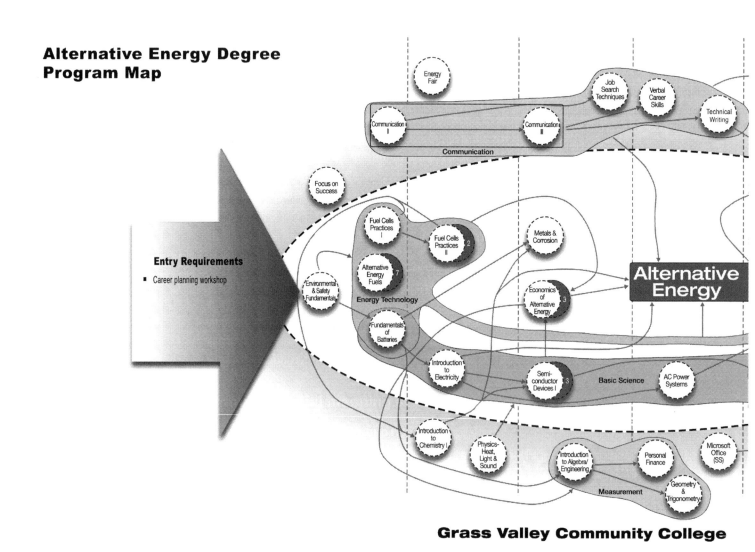

Figure 4: Alternative Energy Degree Program Map (Associate Degree)

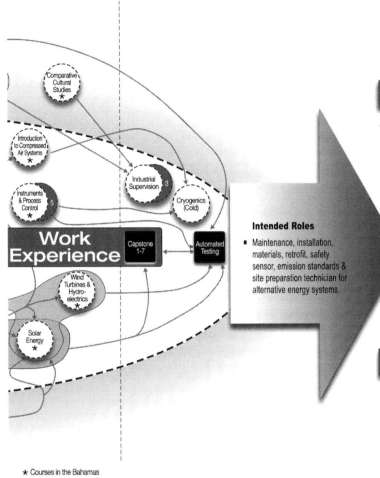

★ Courses in the Bahamas

Intended Roles

■ Maintenance, installation, materials, retrofit, safety sensor, emission standards & site preparation technician for alternative energy systems.

INTENDED LEARNING OUTCOMES

1. Demonstrate effective verbal and written communication skills as an individual and as a team member.

2. Demonstrate basic electrical, mechanical, chemical, mathematical and computer skills involved in maintaining alternative energy systems.

3. Apply sound business and economic principles to achieve and maintain profitability of alternative energy systems.

4. Follow quality and safety procedures.

5. Install, repair and design alternative energy systems.

6. Fabricate and test prototypes.

7. Participate in researching current and emerging alternative energy systems.

ORGANIZATION-WIDE LEARNING OUTCOMES

- Communicate effectively
- Think critically
- Practice from a code of ethics
- Interact well with others
- Show evidence of cultural and global awareness

The Power of Visual Maps

There are few who would argue with the fact that in both college academics and workplace training programs across this country, we waste time and resources when *what we teach* and *how we organize what we teach* isn't based on what learners need. Could it be that we just don't care what learners really need, or that we don't have tools to see the complexities and inefficiencies in the programs we offer?

It has been recently reported that in some institutions of higher education today, it is taking the average learner six years to complete a four-year degree, costing families and society millions of dollars more than it should. Mimicking the same kind of planning that goes on in higher education, workplace educators are still seen *covering content* that in the end doesn't really matter. And, in community colleges, thousands of general education learners are just *taking cours-es* to gather credits without seeing a clear pathway to life-role outcomes.

Few, if any, of these inefficiencies can be blamed on the adult learner. Many can be blamed on our own inability to *see* the disconnect. The problem is we don't have very good tools to help us *see*.

Since the very first human picked up a stick and scratched lines in the dirt guiding others to life-giving water holes and hunting grounds, maps have been powerful learning tools. Whether we scratch them in the dirt, print them on paper or display them on a digital screen, maps do the same things: show us where we have been, show us where we are now and visualize alternate paths to new destinations. Whenever we sense a need to explain structure and movement through space and time, we find ways to create maps.

How many times have we all been asked, "Do I have to draw you a picture?" The answer is "yes," and why not? Maps and other visual images do something that text simply cannot do effectively—they reveal *connections and relationships.* And the key to understanding any dynamic system is seeing connections and relationships in context.

While maps have played a central role in discovering and documenting almost everything in the universe, there has been little application in the practices and processes of education and training at any level. Could this be because our mental image of education is that of *teaching* rather than *learning* and we have failed to recognize that the learners are literally *on a journey*?

This Primer illustrates how we, as educators, can use visual tools to align training and education experiences with learning outcomes that are relevant to the lives of learners. Visual tools give us the power to think more strategically, deal with the complexities of learning assessment, and show greater accountability for the resources we are expending.

Using Maps in Curriculum Planning

Unless we perceive learning as a journey toward defined outcomes, we fail to even think of *a* map as a tool for planning educational programs, courses, and workshops. It is the transition away from an image of an instructor *covering content* to one of learners *moving toward outcomes* that makes a visual *map* a tool of choice wherever learning occurs.

So, what specifically is it that we can map? We can map programs, courses, pathways, departments, concepts, journeys, and even an abstract idea—anything that is composed of connected parts can be mapped. That includes just about everything about learning: mind maps, concept maps, course activity maps, program maps, assessment maps, content maps, and outcome maps. All of these maps are used to make relationships visible— to see all parts of a concept or process and understand what they mean together—something dense text and narrative struggle to do.

Before we present the process for showing how a visual map can be an effective and efficient way to design outcomes and learning assessment at every level of curriculum planning, let's clarify some important terminology that we'll be using throughout this Primer.

Working Definitions

Map: A visual representation that depicts the relationship of different elements, often for the purpose of aiding in navigation.

Program: A highly organized set of learning experiences that learners navigate through and that result in intended learning outcomes. In academic settings, programs are often associated with degrees, diplomas or certificates. In workplace settings, they usually consist of a series of workshops, with some even leading to a certificate or licensure.

Program Map: The organization and visual depiction of the learner's journey through learning experiences and assessments aligned to achieve intended learning outcomes.

Learner's Journey: A flow of learning experiences that learners navigate through to achieve the intended learning outcomes.

Mapping: A process of using visual tools to show the learner's journey of activities and experiences that align with intended learning outcomes.

The Power of the Program Mapping Process

Program mapping is first and foremost a tool for engaging instructors in a conversation about the synergistic nature of a program or workshop series.

It is a tool that can totally change the kind of conversations that have traditionally gone on in curriculum planning meetings. One long-time member of a higher education medical faculty told us, "This is the first time in 20 years of curriculum meetings that I have been involved in a conversation that went deeper than changing course titles and descriptions, approving textbook selections and debating whose turn it was to teach night sections." Obviously there was something significant happening in the program mapping process—something more important.

A few weeks after we facilitated a mapping session in the Northwest, I (Ruth) got a call from the Academic Vice President's office; it was an urgent call. Instructors from the journalism program were frantic because the map they had created was nowhere to be found—they thought I might have it. Two weeks later I got the same call; still no map in sight. How embarrassed I was to find that I had carefully folded it and slipped it into my briefcase. I was doubly embarrassed because of how much value they attached to their map.

The same thing happened more recently after a mapping session at the University of Maryland University College. The English Program's map was misplaced and later found in the Dean's office because it was thought to be such a good example. The lesson we learned is that when instructors invest in creating a program map, they *own* it. What more could we ask for?

The power of program mapping is the conversation it stimulates—a conversation that focuses on resolving strategic and systemic issues like:

- better alignment of both content and learning activities with intended outcomes,
- increased connectivity between courses or workshops; awareness of repetition and transfer of essential content,

- alignment of program capstone experiences and assessment tasks with each other and with the intended outcomes,

- concern for consistent benchmarks and standards across the program, and

- the collection and use of evidence.

We are not alone in seeking to develop tools that challenge traditional training and academic design models. In his book, *Leaving ADDIE for SAM*, Michael Allen proposes a new model that has similarities to software systems such as Agile, Extreme Programming, and SCRUM which uses iteration, short cycles, and other techniques to produce the best learning. Being able to quickly design and develop a successive approximation method (SAM) provides a quick *visual* of what the learning could look and feel like before continuing to invest in the development. Being able to *see* helps everyone get agreement quicker, and expectations are clearer.

It appears the training world may be ready for mapping in a variety of forms.

The Power of Metaphor and Story

Look at any on-line college catalog and it is almost certain you will find the term *learner-centered*, if not in the mission statement itself, then certainly in the statement of values.

Learner-centered is an idea that looks and sounds real good but might not reflect the thinking or practices of training and curriculum developers and instructors, because it's not the picture of learning they hold in their mind's eye. The more common picture is that of a knowledgeable instructor delivering information, preferably through PowerPoint or other media.

It has been our experience that some instructors don't even recognize *learner-centered* when they see it in a face-to-face or virtual environment. This is the reason we use metaphor. Sometimes it is the only way to change the picture that's already in the mind's eye.

It has been our practice since publishing the first edition of *The OUTCOMES Primer,* fifteen years ago, to use the image and story of a natural river to envision learning. The image is one of paddlers, under the direction of a guide, building proficiency and continual progress toward the *take-out* on a stretch of an unpredictable river. Within this image is everything important to learning, like community, challenging tasks, performance assessment, feedback, reflection, data collection, unpredictable (unintended) and predictable (intended) outcomes, and process improvement. It is the natural river metaphor that captures all the essential elements of learner-centered instruction.

So, let's begin to complete this picture. There are seven (7) basic visuals that pertain specifically to this Primer. Other visuals of the same picture emerge in the other Primers in this series.

1. *The Learner's Journey*—A flow of learning experiences that learners navigate through to achieve the intended outcomes in a program, or down a river, from the initial step of learning, the *put-in,* to the culmination of learning, the *take-out.*

2. *Paddle raft*—an inflatable boat where learners actively paddle the raft, rather than being "oared" by a guide; where learning occurs, be that in a face-to-face or virtual setting.

3. *The River (just a section)*—contrary to common river language, paddle rafters never *run a river*—they *run a section of the river.* Any educational or training program is just a section of a life-long river of learning. Much came before, and much will follow.

4. *Put-in*—starting of a new journey— new section of the river that builds on previous learning, whether it is

the first class session in a course or subsequent session.

5. *Rapids*—challenges that provide evidence of what paddlers on a river or learners in a course or workshop can do with what they have learned; assessment tasks.

6. *Capstone rapid*—a culminating challenge where final evidence of learning is gathered and used, be that on a river or a final exam, project, or report to name a few.

7. *Take-out*—ending the journey that becomes the put-in for the next section of the river or a last class or session before moving forward in learning.

Most of these visuals are captured in Figure 5: The Learner's Journey. Many more elements are added in *The GUIDING Primer: Guiding Toward Learning Outcomes*, a companion book in this series.

A closer look at rapids: *On the river* and *in the classroom*, rapids are the challenges learners are asked to work through for assessing learning. The river image reminds us that without rapids there is little energy—no excitement—no challenge for which to prepare. There is little interest in rafting a river where there are no challenges.

On a good run, rapids are strategically distributed throughout the journey with increasing levels of difficulty. As learners demonstrate what they know and what they can do with what they know, they advance to the next rapid. Guides *assess to assist*, and learners self-assess. It's the natural way it happens on the river.

In the language of the river, the final rapid is called a *capstone* (or more colorfully, a boulder garden)—meaning a complex challenge. It's a final rapid that demands all the skills and understanding the rafters have gathered on that section of the river. Getting through a capstone rapid usually requires combining psychomotor skill with cognitive understanding of river dynamics.

When we begin creating a program map of the learner's journey, we will find that *capstones* don't always come at a fixed point near the end of the journey. Sometimes we intentionally distribute small *boulders* along the journey that together make up the *capstone.*

A closer look at the *take-out*: At the *take-out*, learners walk away with the ability to do something new or something better as a direct (and sometimes indirect) result of the proficiency they have developed on the journey. Following the *take-out*, they are able to apply what they have learned to the next *section of their river*, be it in the workplace, family, community or further *schooling.* Meaningful learning outcomes always describe what paddlers are able to do on the *next section* of life's river—because they were successful on this one.

Because so much of our own professional preparation as instructors and trainers focused on what *we do*, it may always be difficult for some of us to think first about what *learners do*. This is why we keep telling ourselves, "It's their journey not ours." The image of the paddle raft helps to keep this ever in our mind. In a paddle raft (in contrast with an oar raft), it is what paddlers do that eventually gets the guide down the river. The work we are called to do is not primarily about us, our position, our comfort. We are hired because we know the river (the content and the discipline) and are asked to guide learners on their journey for their benefit and the benefit of society.

But, of course, we too are in the raft…and ours is a parallel learning journey. We are observing, assessing, experimenting, testing the water, dredging the river from *take-out* to *put-in* and finding new ways to help learners realize intended and unintended outcomes. *As on the river, and in all living systems, the boundaries often blur—as we are all learners on both the same and different journeys.*

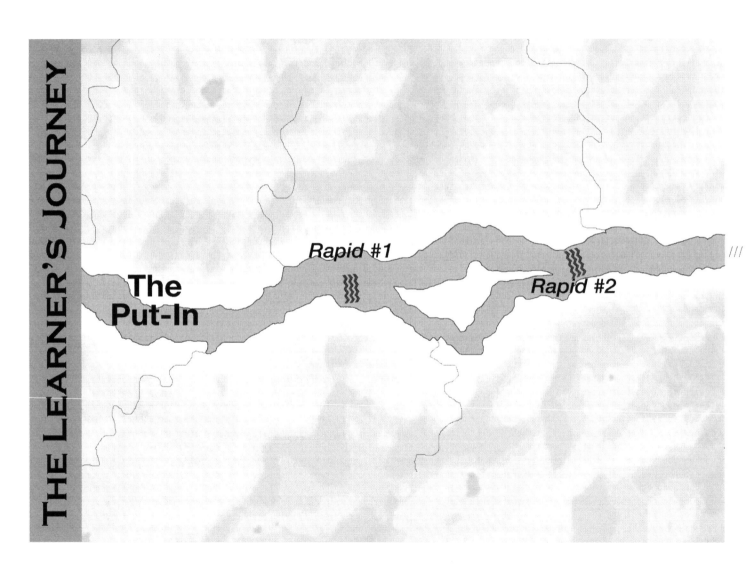

Figure 5: The Learner's Journey

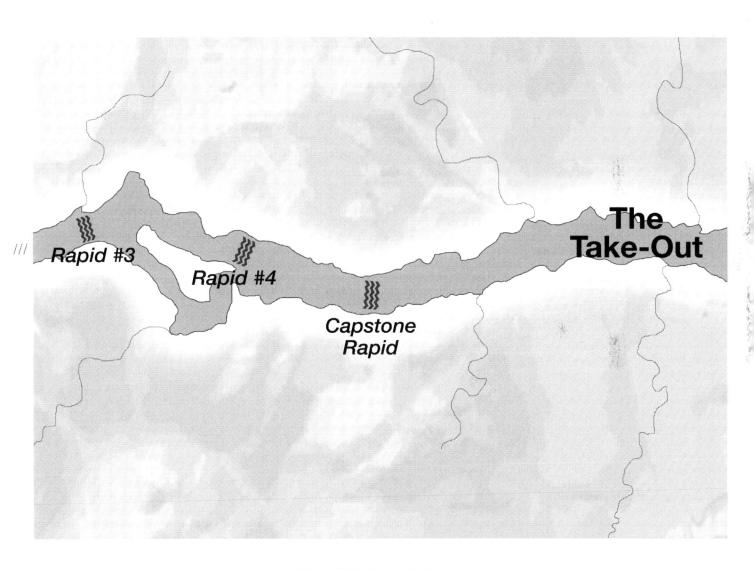

Figure 5: The Learner's Journey

PART TWO
Using Organic Patterns for Curricular Mapping

As people pursue any shared enterprise over time, they develop a common practice, that is, shared ways of doing things and relating to one another that allow them to achieve their joint purpose.

—Fritjof Capra,
The Hidden Connections

Using the Learner's Journey as a Visual Organizer

Because visual mapping is a major departure from the linear way we usually think about curriculum, we begin with a short background about visual patterns prior to introducing the program mapping tool. Being aware of visual patterns helps us understand the breakthrough thinking we will experience in creating program maps.

Using the *learner's journey* as a visual organizer might seem obvious on the surface, but it isn't. Historically and currently, colleges and universities, in particular, are still organized by disciplines and departments; some look a lot like silos of a past agrarian age.

Departments are structured to grow, store and disseminate the stuff they create. The structure of the entire academic side of most colleges elevates distinction over similarities and the knowledge base over learning processes.

Places of work are also most often organized by departments (i.e. Accounting, Human Resources, Marketing, etc.), and workplace training departments are more likely than not to focus on narrow skills without enough knowledge to solve issues as they arise.

As education and training advisors, our team has spent a great deal of time in the past several years talking to top academic officers in colleges and training directors for large firms in the United States and Canada. One thing we have learned is that it is possible to ask some very simple questions that give us quick insights into how organizations "think" about learning.

One of the easier questions we ask college leaders is, "How many programs do you have?" We wait for the answer. Sometimes it takes a long time to get an answer. There is uncertainty because we are not asking about departments and disciplines, nor are we asking just about professional/technical areas. Most often our question is answered with a question, "What do you mean by a program? Is math a program?"

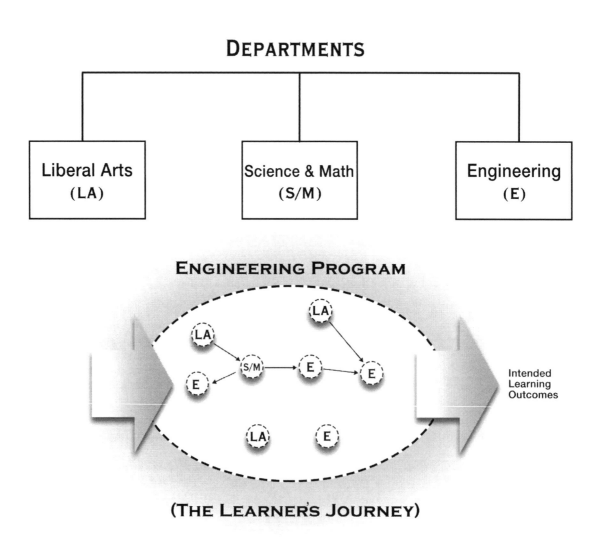

Figure 6: Departments vs. Program

We show the group the image in Figure 6, and say, "An educational *program* is distinguished from an educational *department* in that *a program* consists of a series of learning experiences that learners navigate through to arrive at intended outcomes—most often culminating in a certificate or degree." We repeat it again. "A series of learning experiences that learners navigate through to arrive at intended outcomes." There is more silence.

While we wait for an answer to how many programs they have, let us ask you, the reader, a related question. *Is English (in a typical college) a program under this definition? YES? NO?*

Think again. Do learners typically navigate through all English courses, or do they navigate through a degree or certificate that includes English courses? Even in the case of an English major, the degree *program* is not synonymous with the department. It's a whole different picture.

Failing to get a clear answer for our previous question, we move on to a second question of the head officer, "What work have you already done with learning outcomes?" More often than not, we get a more rapid answer, like, "We have directed our faculty to develop outcome statements for all their courses." This alerts us to the probability that they see courses as islands of knowledge, rather than *tributaries* that converge and feed program level learning outcomes. We see a problem. As long as courses (or workshops) are seen as islands rather than *tributaries* of programs (certificates or degrees), very little thought is being given to the systemic nature of learning. We can further assume that there is little or no need for instructors to talk to each other; they can remain autonomous. No one else needs to touch *their course*. With just these two questions, we begin to see the need for a *program* mapping session.

This traditional picture, that equates learning with department silos, is perhaps the biggest hurdle in our efforts to improve the learner's experience in both colleges and workplace training. It isn't until instructors, administrators, and directors see the organization (the college, the workplace) as a connected and ever changing *system* that outcomes and assessment really make sense.

I (Ruth) saw early evidence of this change of perception not long ago at the very beginning of a mapping session with a large group of instructors. As a place to begin, I simply asked them to list all the courses they taught in their program — it's a place that's usually easy to start. But, in this case, it was several minutes before they quietly admitted they didn't really teach courses. The courses existed on the books, but only to fulfill college and certification requirements. What the learners experienced in their program was one fully integrated learning experience. The experiences they could map, but the experiences weren't seen as isolated courses. In their minds, they had already perfected the flow.

Visual Patterns, Old and New

There are many visual patterns that structure the way we view everything around us. They are the shapes and patterns we learned before we even learned to read. Most of us have at least faint memories of our earliest classroom learning experiences in pre-school, kindergarten or first grade. I (Ruth) distinctly remember the purple ditto on the buff newsprint with the teacher's instructions to "color the circle red, color the square blue, color the triangle yellow, and color the rectangle brown." (I have always liked red best.)

Then there was the ditto worksheet that asked us to identify the apple as a circle, the blue sailboat as a triangle, the frame around the picture of a cat as a rectangle, the orange pumpkin as a circle, the hamster cage as a square and a snowman as a hierarchy of three circles. Snowballs were just smaller circles and building blocks were just smaller squares.

Walking home from school, we learned to see these images everywhere. It was true; the world was made of tidy, discrete shapes. In art class, we were allowed to get messy but, even then, staying inside the line was desirable.

Building on this early recognition of shapes, we learned in our geometry lessons that we could measure these things using the principles and formulas of Euclidian geometry. When we put measuring and counting together with recognizable shapes, we could create a complete picture of the world, or so we thought.

It shouldn't surprise us when we continue to see the world through these limited, tidy shapes. We carry them into the way we perceive organizations to function, while in reality, organizations are living systems where few things are "tidy."

Old School Charts and Hierarchies

Because of these *old school* experiences, more often than not, when we visualize processes, we create flow charts constructed of identical squares made of solid lines; when we picture organizations, we depict a hierarchical series of rectangles, top to bottom (again, with solid lines); when we display data, we cluster it in matrices made of neatly stacked squares or rectangles. We use the triangle to create abstract models of hierarchy; less seldom, we use the circle to depict centers of influence. (Did you just feel that visual shift?)

So far, technology has only reinforced these same graphic patterns of thinking. We can now go to a toolbar and select a line width sufficiently dark to imply an impenetrable boundary. We think thicker lines are better because we think about objects in isolation; thick also denotes boundaries with a clear notion of inside and outside.

It's hard to say how far today's technology has brought us; we still just make our circles red, our squares blue, our triangles yellow, and our rectangles brown while missing the smell of a crayon.

Like all of Western Society, most businesses, agencies, and colleges reinforce traditional ways of thinking with categorization, separation, and hierarchical patterns (top of Figure 7 on page 63). Colleges do it through the very isolation of disciplines (thick boundaries) and discrete segmentation of courses and trainings (squares). Connections are often limited to defined prerequisites and linear sequences. There's little or no resemblance to the patterns we see in living organisms: interdependence, emergence, self-organizing and self-adjusting. These are all patterns we seek to visualize in curricular mapping. In all honesty, very little about outcomes assessment fits into Euclidian mental models at all; it's organic (bottom of Figure 7 on page 63).

Patterns in Living Systems

When did you last see the square, the rectangle or the triangle in a living system? (Is there anything in the living world that has square corners?) The circle (sphere) is different — it's the basic building block of all living things and its boundaries are permeable. It is never isolated, but rather embedded and interdependent. When we look at living systems, we not only see spheres, we see spirals, tubes, layers, binaries, cycles, breaks, bifurcations, networks, branches, centers, dispersed centers, emergence, change, flow, and that wonderful concept of autopoiesis — the ability of living systems to self-organize. These are the visual patterns of the living world.

A good deal has been written in recent years about the recognition of systemic patterns in both natural and social environments. Perhaps the broadest discussion is found in a book by Tyler Volk about the patterns that can be observed throughout the entire universe. In *Metapatterns* (1995), Volk provided a marvelous description of twelve patterns that are detected from the microscopic world to the expanding universe. The value of the work is that Volk crosses all disciplines, and makes us think about everything we see in the world around us as a variation on a relatively simple, yet highly complex, set of patterns. After reading this work, it is impossible to walk down a garden path without seeing the path as a tube (connector), seeing grapes on a vine as spheres, and to realize that the grape and the moon share the same pattern—a pattern that has purpose and function. It's an inspiring book that contributes greatly to our ability to see patterns in living things.

Margaret Wheatley (1996, 2002), an international business consultant and author, has written several books where she has tried to help us all think in some of these same living patterns. Along with Fritjof Capra, author of *The Web of Life* (1996) and *The Hidden Connections* (2002), Wheatley acknowledges the following ways life seems to happen:

"Everything in life is in a constant process of discovery and creation."

"Life uses messes to get to well-ordered solutions."

"Life organizes around identity."

"Life begets more life."

"Everything participates in the creation and evolution of its neighbors."

So here we have contemporary thought leaders crossing the disciplines, thinking and talking about patterns that exist in a living world, patterns that expand our understanding of how things work.

Moving From Euclidian to Organic Shapes

Look again at the two simple illustrations (Figure 7: Visual Patterns of Thinking, page 63). The top diagram represents a very mechanical way of thinking about a process or system. It works well for mechanical tasks, but it doesn't represent well the characteristics of living systems. In contrast, the bottom diagram begins to speak of permeability, emergence, embeddedness, and interdependence.

Pattern Conventions for Curricular Maps

In our description of the mapping elements, you will see evidence of our effort to move you away from boxes and straight lines. You will create permeable circles, messy clusters, flowing lines, spider-like networks, non-linear structures—all in the face of a noticeable absence of boxes.

All the tools described in this book represent a blending of linear and non-linear thinking for an educational system caught up in both the traditions of mechanical thinking and the emergence of organic thinking. To us, these two traditions represent an ever new emerging picture of where we have been (mechanical thinking), with where we are going (organic thinking).

Mechanical Patterns of Thinking - Pre 21st Century

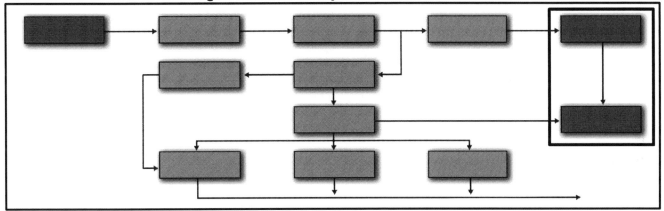

Organic Patterns of Thinking - Post 21st Century

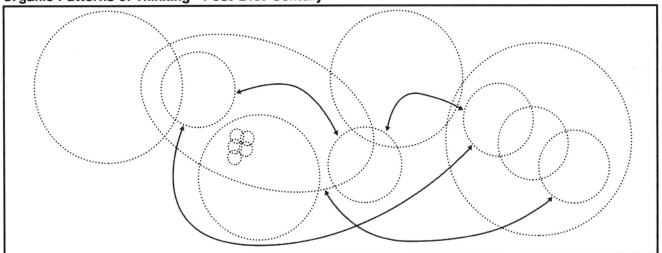

Figure 7: Visual Patterns of Thinking

PART THREE
Preparing Yourself to Create Curricular Maps

A map does not just chart, it unlocks and formulates meaning;
it forms bridges between here and there, between disparate
ideas that we did not know were previously connected.

— Reif Larsen,
The Selected Works of T.S. Spivet

Process or Product?

There are two reasons you will want to map a program. It is hard to say which is more important. The first reason is the *process* itself. When a team gathers around a table to place and arrange all the courses and learning experiences in alignment with the intended program outcomes, questions and issues abound. They are deep questions and issues that never surface when individual trainers and instructors look at courses in isolation. Critical issues surface from the instructors, rather than from management or certification agencies. It is about self-adjustment rather than compliance.

Just as important as the process is the program map itself. It serves as a continual focal point for discussion and captures change over time. Whether program maps remain as Post-it® Notes on a sheet of butcher paper or become colorful digital graphics published on the web, they are the best possible way to communicate the professional integrity of a program and a way to communicate it quickly.

This section answers the questions:
- What are the mapping conventions?
- What are common flow patterns?
- How do program maps evolve?
- How do you adapt the mapping process for a course or workshop?

Exploring Program Mapping Conventions

In developing the graphic conventions for program maps, we have taken care to create a feeling of organic flow in keeping with patterns found in living systems which we wrote about in Part Two. At the same time, the map itself captures the idea of a progressive non-linear journey toward an intended outcome.

You will recall that, as an introduction to this Primer, we flooded you with a whole series of the black pages illustrating each convention used in a program map. We summarize those basic conventions in Figure 8: Overview of Mapping Conventions on the following page. You will want to review these conventions before reading further.

Overview of Mapping Conventions—

 is for
SOCIETY
-the context in which we all live, work, and for which the organization exists.

 is for an
ORGANIZATION
-with a permeable boundary, where energy, resources and information flow continuously to and from the community.

 is for
training or academic PROGRAM
-any organization unit that helps learners move toward intended learning outcomes and identified roles in the community.

 is for
ENTRY
into the program
-the requirements to enter and succeed in the program.

 is for
INTENDED ROLE(S)
after the program
-specific community or employment role(s) or functions that learners are being prepared for in a real-life setting(s) based on the intended learning outcomes (e.g.global citizen, consumer, medical assistant, etc.).

 is for
COURSES or WORKSHOPS
in the program
-learning experiences designed to help the learner achieve intended learning outcomes.

 is for
COURSES or WORKSHOPS
inside the organization but outside the program
-learning experiences offered by other departments and necessary to our intended learning outcomes.

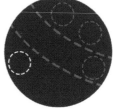 is for
LEARNING EXPERIENCES
outside the organization
-opportunities in the wider community that relate to intended learning outcomes.

Figure 8: Overview of Mapping Conventions (1 of 2)

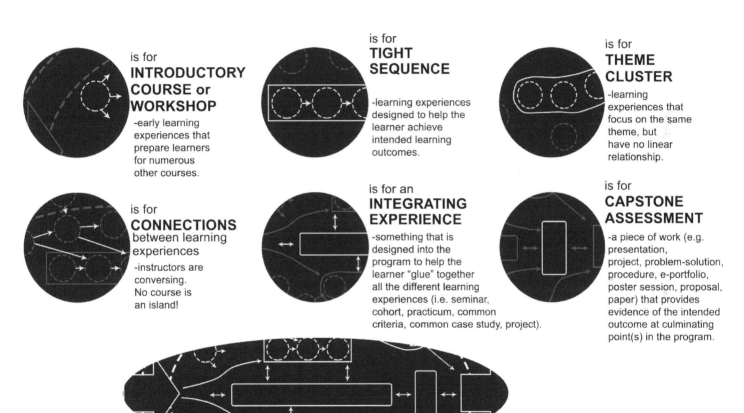

is for
INTRODUCTORY COURSE or WORKSHOP
-early learning experiences that prepare learners for numerous other courses.

is for
TIGHT SEQUENCE
-learning experiences designed to help the learner achieve intended learning outcomes.

is for
THEME CLUSTER
-learning experiences that focus on the same theme, but have no linear relationship.

is for
CONNECTIONS between learning experiences
-instructors are conversing. No course is an island!

is for an
INTEGRATING EXPERIENCE
-something that is designed into the program to help the learner "glue" together all the different learning experiences (i.e. seminar, cohort, practicum, common criteria, common case study, project).

is for
CAPSTONE ASSESSMENT
-a piece of work (e.g. presentation, project, problem-solution, procedure, e-portfolio, poster session, proposal, paper) that provides evidence of the intended outcome at culminating point(s) in the program.

is for
PROGRAM MAP -a systemic view of planned learning experiences - entrance to exit

Figure 8: Overview of Mapping Conventions (2 of 2)

Now look carefully at the conventions as they are incorporated in Figure 4: Alternative Energy Degree Program Map on pages 40–41. You can also download or view this map on our web site: *www.outcomeprimers.com.*

Note: Don't let this map intimidate you. Program maps are not all this complex. This is a final (third generation) map, developed over several months. It has gone through two other stages of evolution before getting to this point. We discuss these stages on pages 83–88.

As you study the map on pages 40–41, read the following description of each element. These are all the elements you will be building into your program maps. The more familiar you are with them, the easier it will be for you to design your own maps using these conventions.

Program Title

The program title is located at the top left corner. You can also add the last revision date. This program, offered by Grass Valley Community College, culminates in an Associate of Applied Science degree in Alternative Energy.

Intended Role(s)

Some kind of role description is essential to envisioning outcomes. Intended roles are embedded in the arrow at the far right of the map to indicate the roles that learners are being prepared for in a real-life setting(s) based on the intended learning outcomes. It represents the *take-out*. The role(s) may be quite general or very specific. In the sample map, they are specific technical roles for which a worker is preparing. Most role descriptions fall into general areas like worker, life-long learner, community member, global citizen, steward of the environment. The intended role(s) is the first thing determined when you want to create a new program. In what specific, or general, life role do we envision them demonstrating the intended outcomes?

Figure 9: Intended Role(s)

Entry Requirements

This arrow, located at the beginning of the map template, represents the *put-in*; it describes specific and/or general qualifications or requirements (if any) the learner must meet prior to entering this program.

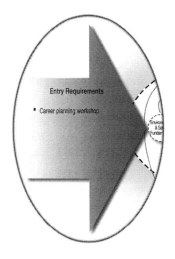

Figure 10: Entry Requirements

Intended Learning Outcome(s)

Outcome statements, located in a list at the far right of the map template, describe what learners will be able to do (in the intended roles) upon completion of this program. These seven very focused program outcomes were generated and validated by a diverse group of persons using the process described in *The OUTCOME Primer:*

Envisioning Learning Outcomes. The statements meet six quality criteria including brevity, clarity, action, context, scope, and complexity.

INTENDED LEARNING OUTCOMES

1. Demonstrate effective verbal and written communication skills as an individual and as a team member.

2. Demonstrate basic electrical, mechanical, chemical, mathematical and computer skills involved in maintaining alternative energy systems.

3. Apply sound business and economic principles to achieve and maintain profitability of alternative energy systems.

4. Follow quality and safety procedures.

5. Install, repair and design alternative energy systems.

6. Fabricate and test prototypes.

7. Participate in researching current and emerging alternative energy systems.

Figure 11: Intended Learning Outcomes

Organization-wide Learning Outcomes

These are general learning outcomes that are intended for learners in all education and training programs across a given organization. Most colleges have general education outcomes and most places of work have

company or agency values that can be reinforced in all training.

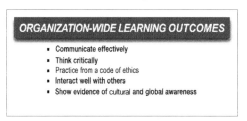

ORGANIZATION-WIDE LEARNING OUTCOMES

- Communicate effectively
- Think critically
- Practice from a code of ethics
- Interact well with others
- Show evidence of cultural and global awareness

Figure 12: Organization-wide Learning Outcomes

Courses/Learning Events

Post-it® Notes (circle shapes preferred), representing courses or workshops, are strategically placed on the map, in some progressive order, and in an area of the map that indicates what part of the organization is responsible for them.

You will notice that all of the courses inside the center boundary are *owned*, or central to that specific program. Supporting courses that are offered by other departments are placed beyond the inner circle. Learning experiences offered by outside organizations are placed beyond the boundaries. You can imagine how tentative this all is in the beginning; the real challenge comes when all the Post-it® Notes are on the paper and everyone seems to have their own idea of where things actually reside. This is expected, and it energizes the discussion.

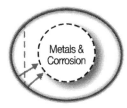

Figure 13: Courses

Introductory Course

An introductory course is easily recognized by its location and by multiple arrows that move downstream.

Figure 14: Introductory Course

Outcome Assessment

Program outcomes are assessed in specific courses. On this program map, a key assessment point (rapid) for an intended outcome is indicated by a color shadow behind the course and contains the number of the intended program outcome that is assessed there. Organization-wide outcomes can be noted with abbreviations such as CT for critical thinking. As you identify how assessment is distributed across the map, you will want to create the colored shadow by placing a different colored Post-it® Note underneath with exposure on the right side. Using a consistent colored Post-it® Note for assessment is essential. (We consistently use green for assessment.)

Figure 15: Outcome Assessment

Sequential courses

Sometimes course sequence doesn't matter, but when it does, the relationship is shown through a direct arrow. A broken line arrow means concurrent enrollment is possible.

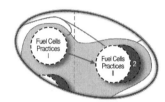

Figure 16: Sequential Courses

Tight Sequence

When we find we have two or more courses that really function as one continuing experience (highly dependent on each other), we draw a box around them. This is a reminder that they should be designed as a whole even though they are separate courses or workshops taught by different people.

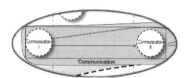

Figure 17: Tight Sequence

Theme Clusters

Learning experiences that need not be sequential are often related in another way; they share the same theme, and therefore, lead to the same program outcome. This is illustrated by a shaded field of any shape or size.

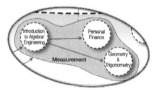

Figure 18: Theme Clusters

Integrated Experience

Sometimes programs have an integrated experience to help the learners glue together what they have learned in separate courses or workshops (e.g. cohort, internship, case study, project, etc.). It is shown as a long rectangle on this map with all the related connections identified.

Integrated experiences are usually found to the right of center because they synthesize and apply what has been learned in previous courses; they are often designated as a capstone assessment point.

Figure: 19: Integrating Experience

Capstone Course

A capstone assessment is a final assessment point (rapid) for more than one of the intended outcomes of the program, and can be a separate class or integrated into a practicum or project. In this map, it is part of the work experience. All seven of the program outcomes are assessed at this point, even though they had been assessed in earlier courses. Wherever they occur, they are visually highlighted through color (green) and a soft-colored square or rectangle.

Figure 20: Capstone Course

Organization-wide Course

Colleges, in particular, have general courses that are often part of the learner's journey through many different programs. These learning experiences may or may not lead to program outcomes, but they do lead to learning outcomes at the organization-wide level.

On the program map, these courses are shown outside the program's boundary (the oval). They provide a different kind of challenge that is in context.

Figure 21: Organization-wide Course

Learning Experiences Outside the Organization

When we *zoom out*, we often see that there are great learning experiences beyond what the organization offers that can contribute to the intended program outcomes. These experiences are identified and placed at the outer edge of the map and have a connection to theme clusters or specific courses. The Energy Fair is shown in the upper left, but while it is noted on the map, no connections seem to be made with any of

the learner's other experiences. These are the kinds of insights a good map provides that may lead to a better use of learning resources that exist outside the program.

Figure 22: Outside the Organization

Seeding Common Flow Patterns

As any experienced facilitator will tell you, in addition to the established conventions, there are some basic flow patterns that repeatedly emerge in the mapping process. Some facilitators find it helpful to *seed* these patterns either during or before the mapping process. For example, it might become obvious that the sequencing of courses is a straight, linear line with no other possible option. Each one must follow the other. It looks and feels like a daisy chain, so that's what we call it. "I think you have a daisy chain."

Here is a quick depiction of five common flow patterns that we see in program maps, more than one of which can appear on the same map for a combination of flow patterns.

—Theme Cluster

What it says: "common theme." Clusters of courses often emerge around themes or skill areas on a map with little or no specificity of order or sequence. Beyond course titles, clusters are identified with a name that aligns with one or more intended program outcome(s). Clusters of courses in a program that have a common theme but are not necessarily taken in sequence are often shown as a set of dotted circles within an amoeba-shaped elongated circle (as was shown in Figure 18, page 74).

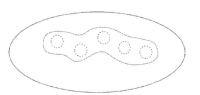

Figure 23: Theme Cluster

—Daisy Chain

What it says: "mandated order." Each course must build on the previous one—common with technical and skill-building content. Some highly sequential programs will show a flow pattern of parallel daisy chains. These flow patterns are also identified as tight sequences (as was shown in Figure 17, page 74).

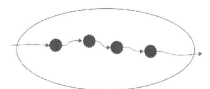

Figure 24: Daisy Chain

—Daisy Wheel

What it says: "no specific direction." There is no prescribed sequence to the experiences. The learner can go in any of the multiple directions. Nothing necessarily builds on anything else. This is often found in liberal arts programs.

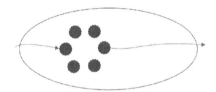

Figure 25: Daisy Wheel

—Integrator

What it says: "synthesize and apply." The best daisy wheels *("no specific direction")* often have at the core an experience (seminar, project, theme. . .) that brings learning into context.

Practicums, major projects, theses, and internships are all significant integrators into which a variety of learning experiences may flow. When we see a daisy wheel emerging, we hope to see an integrator.

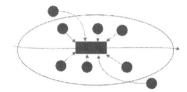

Figure 26: Integrator

—Kettle Pond

What it says: "disconnected." When ice fields pull back, they leave small isolated ponds of fresh water which stay around until no one remembers why they exist. Such is the required course that may no longer align with any program outcomes; nothing flows in or out. Kettle ponds are easy to spot on a program map and give reason for concern.

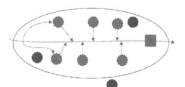

Figure 27: Kettle Pond

Summary of Common Flow Patterns

–Theme Cluster What it says: "common theme." Clusters of courses often emerge around themes or skills areas on a map with little or no specificity of order or sequence. Beyond course titles, clusters should be identified with a theme that aligns with the intended program outcomes.	
–Daisy Chain What it says: "mandated order." Each course must build on the previous one—common with technical and skill building content. Some highly sequential programs will show a flow pattern of parallel daisy chains.	
–Daisy Wheel What it says: "no specific direction." There is no prescribed sequence to the experiences. The learner can go in any of the multiple directions. Nothing necessarily builds on anything else.	
–Integrator What it says: "synthesize and apply." The best daisy wheels have something at the core—an experience (course, seminar, project,...) that brings learning into context. Practicums, major projects, theses, and internships are all significant integrators into which many other learning experiences flow.	
–Kettle Pond What it says: "disconnected." When ice fields pull back, they leave small isolated ponds of fresh water which stay around until no one remembers why they exist. Such is the required course that may no longer align with any program outcomes; nothing flows in or out.	

Figure 28: Summary of Common Flow Patterns

Expecting Program Maps to Evolve Through Stages

We have discovered that program maps tend to evolve through three significant stages. We refer to them as Gen 1, Gen 2, and Gen 3 maps. Each evolution seems to serve quite different purposes which we will explore in this section. But, before we can even begin creating a Gen 1 map, we need to address the relationship between program maps, program outcomes, and a program outcome guide.

Program Outcomes

How to write effective learning outcome statements is beyond the scope of this primer. But, because everything else depends on quality outcome statements, we have devoted an entire primer to that purpose—*The OUTCOME Primer: Envisioning Learning Outcomes.*

Normally, it is best to improve learning outcomes before developing a program map, but it isn't an absolute ne-cessity. It is important to at least be able to recognize good and bad outcomes because weaknesses will become mighty obvious in the mapping process. You can map courses and workshop sequences that already exist, but you can't test them against outcomes that aren't there at all or are poorly written.

There are definite times when creating a program map is helpful before perfecting learning outcome statements . . . meaning, before you really know what you want learners to achieve. It can work for you when you have an existing program and a team of instructors who see no reason to change anything. Here are the three conditions under which we like to map a program *before* spending a lot of time trying to perfect outcome statements.

1. Instructors have little or no interest in developing outcome statements.

2. Instructors have a history of being autonomous and do not discuss

with each other their courses or the learner's journey.

3. Instructors are resistant to doing things together and in the past have seen few results.

Starting with mapping the program first will work under these conditions because the mapping process itself will raise the need for better outcomes.

The Program Outcome Guide

If you have completed a *pogging work-session* as described in *The CONTENT Primer: Aligning Essential Content with Learning Outcomes*, you should have a Program Outcome Guide (POG). It contains some of the critical parts that need to be on your map (outcomes, assessment tasks, and essential content). For your reference, Figure 29, on the following page, shows the critical parts of a POG that has been developed from the program

map, Figure 4, back on pages 40–41.

If you don't have a POG, you can still begin building a map. However, it will only be a glimpse of what currently exists in your program, and may neither raise nor answer the questions concerning what concepts, skills, and issues need to be learned. Instead of a Gen 1 map, perhaps we would have to call yours a Pre-map.

POG/COG/WOG TITLE: POG: Alternative Energy Degree Program   **Date:** _____

Concepts & Issues	Skills	Assessment Tasks	Intended Outcomes
What must the learners understand to demonstrate the intended outcome?	*What skills must the learners master to demonstrate the intended outcome?*	*What will learners do in here to demonstrate evidence of the outcome?*	*What do learners need to be able to DO "out there" in the rest of life that we're responsible for "in here"?*
-Energy sources: solar, wind, fuel cells -Fossil fuels -Heat transfer -Chemical reaction -Power systems -Energy consumption -Photovoltaic systems -Hydro-electricity -Energy quantification -Electrolysis -PEM (proton exchange membrane) -Convection current -Kinetic energy -Evaluation models -Site Assessments	1. Argue for the pros and cons of alternative energy. 2. Classify alternative energy resources by use, availability, and environmental impact. 3. Analyze energy systems according to efficiency, economics, and environment. 4. Design, fabricate and test prototypes. 5. Apply science principles of electronics, chemistry, physics, mechanics to design and test systems. 6. Conduct laboratory experiments. 7. Work safely and use personal protection equipment. 8. Contribute responsibly to the efforts of a team. 9. Evaluate energy systems.	1. Write position papers and make presentations on the pros and cons of at least three alternative energy systems: wind, solar, and fuel cells. 2. Assess renewable energy resources for residential and commercial customers in wind, solar, and fuel cells. 3. Individually conduct a site assessment with specific recommendations based on data. 4. Design residential and commercial energy systems in wind, solar, and fuel cells based on a comprehensive assessment and customer requirements. 5. Install, maintain, and troubleshoot alternative energy systems.	1. Demonstrate effective verbal and written communication skills as an individual and team member. 2. Demonstrate basic electrical, mechanical, chemical, mathematical and computer skills involved in maintaining alternative energy systems. 3. Apply sound business and economic principles to achieve and maintain profitability of alternative energy systems. 4. Follow quality and safety procedures. 5. Install, repair, & design alternative energy systems. 6. Fabricate and test prototypes. 7. Participate in researching current and emerging alternative energy systems.
-Safety (self, community, environment) -Feasibility of systems -Return on Investment			

What issues must the learners be able to resolve to demonstrate the outcome?

Figure 29: Alternative Energy Degree Program Outcome Guide

First Generation Maps (Gen 1)

Creating a first generation program map is primarily a task of getting all the existing learning experiences (courses, workshops, prerequisites, practicums, entry level requirements, learning outcomes) down on individual Post-it® Notes, placing them on a program map template and tentatively aligning them with program outcomes.

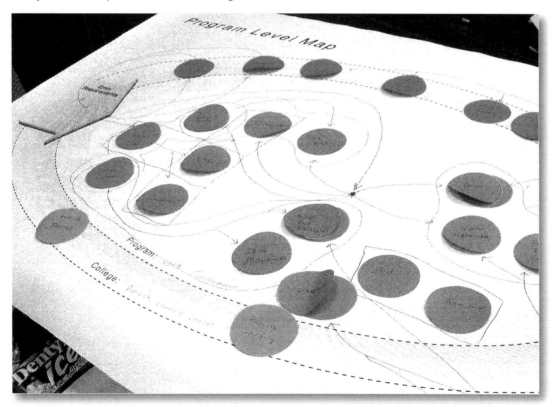

Figure 30: First Generation Program Map

In an existing program, where instructors sometimes feel they *own* their courses, it is highly beneficial to have all instructors involved at the outset. They like to put their *own* courses on the map — where they think they belong. And it needn't take a great deal of time to do this. In as little time as one hour, you will be able to put together an initial map that will energize instructors, raise a lot of questions and generate a sense of urgency to move ahead. The questions will be many:

"How does that course fit?"

"Why do we have that outcome statement?"

"Where is that outcome assessed — or isn't it assessed?"

"Why does that course come so late?"

"Where do we gather that evidence?"

"How does that course contribute to these outcomes?"

"Do we need to re-consider these outcomes?"

"Maybe we should think about a capstone course?"

"Where do we address the organization-wide learning outcomes? What are they?"

Second Generation Maps (Gen 2)

Gen 2 program maps are the ones that keep us intellectually honest. The task is to answer the questions raised in the process of creating the first map and to incorporate changes in Gen 2 maps that improve the program, provide more detail to the Gen 1 map, and make it a useful tool for program review, advising, and even staffing. If it is still a work in progress, it can always be changed. As these changes are shared with others, they are gathering further input for additional modifications and changes. In all honesty, some Gen 2 maps are never turned into Gen 3 maps. They remain a work in progress. That's fine.

When creating Gen 2 maps, an example of which is shown in Figure

31, you can expect many questions to surface. We have provided Questions to Guide the Conversation for Second Generation Mapping (Figure 32 on page 86). Select the ones you think are important and and raise them. (Note carefully that this Gen 2 map is a different program than the Gen 1 map shown in Figure 30.)

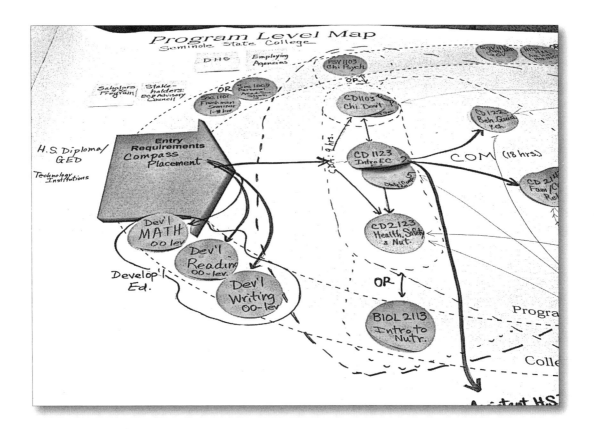

Figure 31: Second Generation Map

Questions to Guide the Conversation for Second Generation Mapping

A primary purpose of program mapping is to help us see the program as a whole which generates new ideas for strengthening the learning experience. The conversation that took place while creating your first generation map should have already pointed to specific concerns and ideas for change.

Entry Requirements

- Are the entry requirements adequate?
- Do we have control over specifying the entry requirements?
- Colleges only: Are the developmental courses, if needed, shown on the map?

Intended Role(s)

- Are the role(s) appropriate for this program?
- Colleges only: Are the roles broad enough to encompass the general education component of the program?

Intended Learning Outcomes

- Are the program outcome statements significant as they relate to the intended role?
- Do the program outcomes provide a clear direction of intent and inclusiveness?
- Do the statements paint a clear picture of what learners should be able to do with what they have learned in real-life contexts?
- Do the program learning outcomes align with the organization-wide learning outcomes?

College	Workplace
Communicate effectively	Communication
Demonstrate critical thinking	Quality
Community, cultural and global awareness	Respect
Maintain a code of ethics	Integrity

Courses and Other Learning Experiences

- How does each course shown contribute to the intended learning outcome(s)?
- Is the amount of time (credit) given to each course appropriate to achieve the intended learning outcome(s)?
- What essential learning experiences might be missing?
- Do any courses appear to be disconnected? Why do we have them?
- Are appropriate introductory courses specified? Does the map show how they contribute to success in subsequent courses?

Figure 32: Questions to Guide the Conversation for Second Generation Mapping (continues next page)

Key Assessment

- Does the map reveal the primary place each of the program outcomes are assessed and the data tracked? *(This does not mean where they are taught, but rather where they are finally assessed for documentation purposes.)*
- Does the map reveal which course(s) will also assess the organization-wide learning outcomes?

Capstone Assessment

- Is there a current capstone course or experience that integrates learning and provides for final assessment? Should there be?
- Have we agreed upon what the capstone experience should be?
- For which outcomes does the capstone provide learning evidence?
- Is there an agreed upon assessment tool (rubric, scoring guide or test) for the capstone? Who establishes the criteria for the capstone assessment?

Sequencing of Learning Experiences

- Should anything be changed with regard to the flow or sequencing of the courses? Is there evidence to support such a change?
- Would learners make better progress if there were a more defined sequence where learning builds on other learning?
- To guard against reducing access for learners, have optimum sequences been identified?

Connections/Interdependencies Within the Organization

- How strong are the connections between course work and practicums?
- What other educators or programs might we be more closely connected with to improve learning experiences?
- *College only*: Which organization-wide learning outcomes need to be reinforced in our program courses?
- Have we identified a common set of standards to be applied for basic skill development?
- What are learners learning in basic skill development courses that we need to reinforce in our courses?

Integration of Learning

- What provisions have we made in our program for learners to integrate/apply what they are learning throughout the program?
- Have we identified the best possible flow of learning experiences to maximize integration with external activities?

Use of External Learning Opportunities Outside the Organization

- What provisions have we made for identifying and partnering with appropriate agencies and businesses to expand learning opportunities?
- Are all partners shown on the map?

Backup and Redundancy

- Have we digitally photographed all our maps with high resolution equipment to preserve accuracy and integrity?
- Has all computer rendering been standardized and made available to educators and others as appropriate?
- Have provisions been made for standardized multiple digital backup copies of all work? Are they located in a readily identifiable place?

Note: For additional assistance on assessment, consult *The ASSESSMENT Primer: Assessing and Tracking Evidence of Learning Outcomes.*

Third Generation Maps (Gen 3)

Gen 3 program maps are usually produced after all changes to the program are made and approved. Figures 1–4 pages 34–41 are third generation maps.

To see how much you have learned about the conventions used in mapping programs, we suggest you take the time to review one of these maps using the Scoring Guide—Assessing the Quality of a Program Map (Figure 33, on the following page). It will help you see all the connections that are essential in a good map. This scoring guide can also help you assess the maps you construct.

Third generation maps are useful in a program website and printed on materials for learners and advisors who benefit from seeing an entire program illustrated in a comprehensive way. When used on a website, the Program Map can serve as a link to further details on any aspect of the program including course and assessment details at the touch of a finger.

Some colleges find great benefit in requiring that a proposed program change be accompanied by a program map that shows the impact of the change in the context of the whole. And we all know, there is nothing that will support a change proposal better than one visual that can replace a thousand words.

Template: Scoring Guide—Assessing the Quality of a Program Map

Characteristics of Good Program Maps				Suggestions for Improvement
Rating scale: 1=absent 2=present	1	2		
1. Use of Conventions				
Map includes the following basic descriptions: • Program name • Organization name/logo • Date • Entry requirements • Intended roles • Intended learning outcomes (program or organization-wide) Separate colors are used to distinguish types of courses (learning experiences) according to the map legend.				
Rating scale: 1=absent 2=present 3=changes needed	1	2	3	
2. Learning Experiences				
Where learning experiences (courses) are placed on the map reveals where they are offered in relation to the whole organization.				
3. Interdependencies				
The map clearly illustrates how courses interrelate (whether linear or nonlinear). These relationships are expressed through tight sequences, theme clusters, and directional arrows.				
4. Integration of Learning				
Careful consideration has been given to appropriately illustrate any integrative learning experience.				
5. Capstone Assessment				
It is clear where each program learning outcome and organization-wide learning outcome is being assessed.				

Figure 33: Scoring Guide—Assessing the Quality of a Program Map

The last thing we can give you before introducing the Facilitator's Guide to Mapping Programs are some common questions and answers you will probably face. Here are the most important ones.

Common Questions about Curricular Mapping

When is the best time to map a new program?

The *best* time to create a map for a brand new program is *after* you have identified the intended roles and learning outcomes, have completed a Program Outcome Guide (POG) and are beginning to consider what learning experiences (courses) will lead to the intended outcomes. Creating a complete map will guide you through the decisions you will need to make about every aspect of the program—courses, prerequisites, key assessment points, capstone assessments, intended outcomes, entry requirements, and intended roles.

When is the best time to map an existing program?

The best time to map an existing program is the same time you prune roses—NOW! This is because *it is better to prune than not to prune.* Since curriculum reconstruction is a non-linear, iterative process, mapping the program isn't something you do just once. It is something you keep adjusting over time based on learning evidence.

For programs that have existed for a long time, it is usually best to create a *before* map—prior to even reviewing your intended outcomes. Seeing the big picture will raise issues that may need to be addressed. Subsequent discussions will clarify why each course exists, how each course contributes to the outcomes (program and organization-wide level), where major assessment points will be implemented, what capstone experience will synthesize the learning, and how learners will flow through the program.

Who should participate in mapping a program?

The real question is, "Who knows this program best?" More likely than not, it will be those who teach and advise learners in the program. They should do the mapping.

You will recall that we advocated for more diverse representation to identify program learning outcomes. Again, the question was simply, "Who knows it best?" Individuals from other programs and stakeholders in society provide important perspectives on intended outcomes. This kind of broad input is less necessary in aligning learning experiences with already established outcomes.

Do we need a facilitator?

Using a facilitator who is experienced with program mapping will save a great deal of time and energy. When we work with organizations that haven't yet mapped programs, we identify persons with good facilitation skills and train them to facilitate mapping sessions.

Can the facilitator work with more than one program at a time?

The answer is yes, with experience. We don't recommend this on the first try. When we work with college programs, we often have four or even as many as eight different program groups in one large room mapping at the same time. The challenge for the facilitator is giving very clear instructions to multiple teams and getting around to assist each team. A facilitator, if experienced, needs to be skilled in directing multiple groups at once. We have found that there are definite advantages in having the facilitator work with several different programs together in one room:

1. The energy in the room is greater and tends to be contagious.

2. Participants become familiar with programs they never knew existed and get ideas for improving their own program.

3. Facilitator work is increased, but facilitator time is reduced (which may

be an important factor if the facilitator is under contract to do the work).

4. Teams have the opportunity to *display* what they have created with other programs in the same organization. The synergy is quite surprising.

Can you map a course?

There are various ways to show a learner's journey through a course. We show here two approaches. A course map showing the key assessments required of learners is shown in Figure 34, page 94. Another approach is to use a template, as shown in Figure 35, page 95. The first one simply maps the key assessments as they align with the intended learning outcomes, and the second one aligns course content with assessment tasks and learning outcomes. Figure 35 is really a table, not a visual map in the sense of how we have used it in this Primer.

In developing a course map or using a template, as shown in Figures 34 and 35 (pages 94 and 95), you first would refer back to a Course Outcome Guide (COG) that contains the core essential concepts, skills, issues, and assessment tasks for the entire course and determine when these will be taught. Both Figure 34 and 35 show how the weeks have been clustered and what tasks learners are required to complete (e.g., Week 1–3, 4–6, etc.). You can then check the alignment and make adjustments, if necessary.

You can map learning activities to see how they integrate concepts, skills, and issues. Remember, a map is simply a picture of the learner's journey, and however you want to draw that map will probably be better than not having a map at all.

For planning short workshops, mapping may take an even simpler form. It might take the form of something I (Ruth) have always done. Using a large (but not as large) sheet of paper and smaller Post-it® Notes, I design workshops by first writing the outcomes (what I hope the participants will be able to do as a result of attending) on the far right-hand side of the paper. Then I quickly list a variety of learner activities on Post-it® Notes, moving them around until the flow seems to work. Notice how different this is from listing the topics I want to *cover* in a presentation. This planning process with Post-it® Notes helps me keep focused on the intended outcomes for the workshop, and the learner's experience. It is learner-centered, strategic, and, best of all, simple.

In Part Four, we return to program mapping and a step-by-step action guide for facilitating the process.

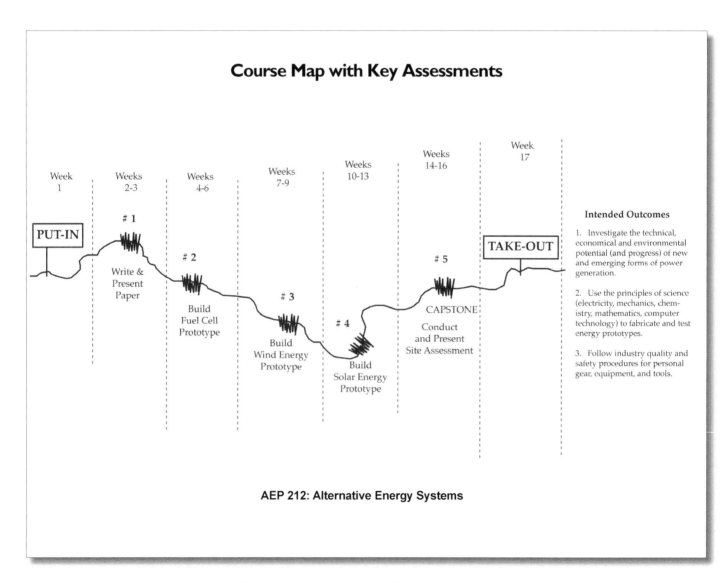

Figure 34: Course Map with Key Assessments

Activity Map	AEP 212: Alternative Energy Systems				
	Week 1–3	Week 4–6	Week 7–9	Week 10–13	Week 14–16	Week 17
Develop a deep understanding of these major concepts	–history of energy consumption –principles of sciences (mechanics, chemistry, electricity) –electro-chemical reactions –fossil fuels –energy quantification	–fuel cells –electrolysis –PEM (proton exchange membrane) –hydro-electricity –chemical reactions –hydro-electric power generation	–wind energy –wind turbines –thermodynamics –convection current –wind factors: speed & temperature –kinetic energy –distributed energy generation systems	–solar energy –electric connectivity –PV (photovoltaic cells) –modules –arrays –thermal heat/energy –cogeneration	–energy evaluation models –integration of energy systems –site assessments	–feedback from instructor on course assessment tasks and assignments
Face these issues	–Feasibility: technical, economic, and environmental	–Safety: self, community, and environment	–Laboratory safety –Team relationships	–Return on Investment	–Return on Investment	
Master these skills	How to: –develop sound arguments for the pros and cons of energy systems –write a good position paper –use statistics to support position on energy systems –contribute equally to work team	How to: –classify energy resources –analyze energy systems –conduct lab experiments –assure safety –contribute to work of the team	How to: –fabricate and test wind turbine prototype –analyze "return on investment" of wind energy systems –conduct lab experiments –interact positively and safely with lab partners	How to: –critically evaluate a solar energy system –observe/examine/ record findings of heat loss –design feasible solutions to energy problems	How to: –accept feedback –plan and organize a site assessment –compile quantitative, qualitative analyses –write a report –conduct energy assessments and interpret energy uses	How to: –self-assess performance –give peer and instructor feedback –make adjustments in learning –apply learning to one's personal life situation
Show Learning Proficiency (Key Assessments)	**–Submit position paper of an energy system and make a 15-minute presentation (wk. 3)**	**–Build prototype of fuel cell system (wk. 6)**	**–Build prototype of wind energy system (wk. 9)**	**–Build prototype of solar energy system (wk. 13)**	**–Develop report & presentation of energy site assessment with proposed solutions (wk. 16)**	**–Complete course evaluation**

Figure 35: Course Activity Map

PART FOUR

Mapping Programs:
A Facilitator's Guide

*Coming together is the beginning; keeping
together is progress; working together is success.*

—*Henry Ford*

Mapping at the program level needs to be facilitated by someone who knows the process and can lead one or more groups through it. With enough facilitators, an organization can map the current state of all their programs and general education disciplines in a multiple day event. They can then be examined and the future state of the program/discipline can be mapped in order to plan the changes that need to be made. This section answers these questions:

- How do I facilitate a program or discipline mapping session?
- What goes into a first generation, second generation and/or third generation map?
- What are the best practices for conducting multiple mapping teams?

First Generation Program Mapping
(Approximately 2 hours)

Purpose

The purpose of constructing the first generation of a program map is to *get a glance* of the learner's entire journey through multiple courses or workshops that comprise a certificate or degree program. This rough (even messy) map will have enough substance to raise issues about access, sequencing, relevance, flow, and alignment of courses with learning outcomes and their related assessment tasks.

Note to Colleges: This process can be adapted to map the sequencing of courses in a single discipline, rather than a certificate or degree. Establishing discipline-based learning outcomes and identifying how each course aligns with those outcomes will be valuable to all programs that share those courses.

Preparation

1. Determine how many programs (or disciplines) you are going to work with at one time.
   If this is your first experience, consider facilitating only one program (or discipline) at a time. With some practice, you can expect to be able to eventually work with several groups which will expose them to each other's work and contribute to the interdisciplinary conversation. When you do map more than one at a time, prepare an assistant or two to help you. You will need a map for each program (or discipline).

2. Decide on the materials you want to use.
   Whiteboards or paper? The downside of the whiteboard is that you can't roll it up and take it out of the room. We prefer to do our mapping on a large (36 x 60 inch) paper map with the basic conventions already printed. We have placed a template in the Appendix of this Primer for scanning and a PDF file on our web site at *www.outcomeprimers.com*. Feel free to copy and enlarge either image.

   Marker or pencil? Use pencil at first to draw flow lines keeping everything flexible as long as possible. Trace the lines later with a fine point marker to make them more visible.

3. Gather your materials.
   Here is what each team will need:

   - One large map or whiteboard
   - Pencils and erasers
   - Sharpie® pens (fine point) to highlight lines when work is finished
   - Approximately 50 3-inch Post-it® Notes (use round ones if you can find them) in 4 different colors—allotting 30 to one color, 5 to another, 15 to another and 8 to another
   - Program and course descriptions
   - Program (or discipline) learning outcomes (if you have them)
   - Organization-wide learning outcomes (if you have them)
   - Sample Program Map for each participant or group

4. Schedule the timeframe.
   Allow at least two (2) hours for the initial mapping process. When you work with more than one group at a time, schedule a three-hour work session to accommodate *show-and-tell* at the end.

5. Invite the participants.

   If this is an existing program, invite everyone who directs or teaches in the program. You can also include adjunct instructors/trainers and one or two learners.

6. Arrange the room.

   Try to arrange the room so the team can comfortably stand or sit around the map. By doing the work on the wall, rather than on a flat table, everyone can see the whole map as it emerges and no one must look at it upside down. Having the group stand around the map also seems to generate greater energy and fuller participation.

Introduce the work

1. Be sure the team members understand why they are mapping their program (to see how learning experiences are connected).

2. Introduce the mapping conventions. Illustrate each of the conventions on a flip chart or distribute a copy of Figure 8: Overview of Mapping Conventions, see pages 68–69.

3. Let the team study and discuss the sample map you have distributed. Choose one from pages 34–41 (Figures 1–4) or provide one you might already have from your organization.

Get them started

1. Gather the team members around their large map.

2. Add the name of the organization and the program. Discuss and add the entry requirements (inside the Entry Requirements arrow) and the role or function for which the learner is preparing (inside the Intended Roles arrow).

3. Post the outcome statements. Have the group write these program outcome

statements in large letters to the far right of the map, outside the organization boundary. If they are already in print in a catalog or website, copy and attach them to the map with tape. If you have organization-wide learning outcomes include them under the program learning outcome statements. *If the outcome statements haven't been written, they will be added later.*

4. Have the team write the course name or an abbreviated title of all *major courses* or workshops on separate Post-it® Notes including the course or workshop number, if there is one. *Note: Distinguish core or major courses by using this same color Post-it® Note.*

5. Have the team roughly place the courses on the map as they envision the learner moving through the program from left to right.

6. Using a different color of Post-it® Notes, write the names of all other courses or workshops included in this certificate or degree program. This will include courses or workshops taught by other departments, but required of learners completing this program. *Note to colleges: This includes skill development and general education requirements.*

7. Now, roughly arrange these courses in the organization perimeter, inside the outer circle. In the case that specific courses or workshops cannot be identified, have the team specify the number of credits or hours that must be completed and a working title rather than a specific course name and number.

8. Using the same color of Post-it® Notes, write the names of support sites or learning opportunities outside the organization (in the community). Many programs depend on outside agencies or services for learning experiences like internships. Identify these on Post-it® Notes and place them either inside or outside the organization.

9. Identify any capstone assessment experience(s) that now exist. A final capstone course or workshop is where learners synthesize what they have learned and provide evidence of the learning outcomes.

10. Use another different color of Post-it® Notes to distinguish any capstone experience. If there isn't a capstone experience, a blank Post-it® Note can be placed where one might be appropriate in the future.

Help them begin to refine their map

Materials—Copy and distribute Figure 28: Summary of Common Flow Patterns on page 79.

Ask the group to:

1. Decide which general flow pattern their program most resembles.
2. Rearrange the Post-it® Notes and add pencil lines and arrows to show how the learning experiences are connected.
3. Seed any questions into their discussion.

> - Are there prerequisite courses? If so, how are they shown? What subsequent courses do they feed into?
> - Are there skill building courses that should be completed early? If so, in what courses are those skills used or reinforced?
> - Do any of the courses form a tight sequence? If so, box them.
> - Do any of the courses form a theme cluster? If so, cluster and circle them (moving them closer together).
> - How are the external resources connected? Draw appropriate arrows.

4. Record emerging issues as they arise. Use Figure 36: Emerging Issues List (page 112) for this purpose. These can be reviewed and the team can determine who should be involved in each issue and a target date for completion.

Look for what integrates the learning experience—the central integrator

An increasing number of programs have something besides courses/workshops that help learners integrate what they are learning as they move through the requirements. Sometimes it is a cohort of learners who move through the program supporting each other; other times it is a theme, case study, practicum or ongoing project that runs throughout the entire program. Whatever it is, have the team place it in the center of the map with other experiences flowing in and out of it. See Alternative Energy Work Experience, page 40, Figure 4: *Alternative Energy Degree Program Map.*

Indicate where key assessments occur

To indicate where evidence of each outcome is gathered (key assessment tasks), have the team place a different colored Post-it® Note behind the course so it shows as a shadow on the right side. Write the corresponding number of the program outcome as well as any organization-wide learning outcome on that shadow. You can assign symbols for each organization-wide learning outcome, such as CO for communication, CT for critical thinking, and other abbreviations as needed.

Bring this initial mapping session to a close

1. Review what the group has accomplished.
2. Have the team use their Emerging Issues List (Figure 36 on page 112) to create an agenda for further work on their map.
3. Have them decide where they will post the map for anyone to attach notes. Make the map a visual focus for conversations over several days. It is important to keep it fluid.

4. Retain and share the map using a digital camera, making sure to take several close-ups to make the details legible.

5. Announce a second mapping work session, if needed. If the plan is to develop the GEN 1 map created here into a GEN 2 map, proceed with the guidelines in the following pages. Otherwise, end the facilitation process, thanking all those who attended.

Second Generation Program Mapping

Purpose

The purpose of second generation mapping is to discuss and resolve issues that may have emerged during or since the first mapping session in the interest of improving the whole learner's experience (i.e. flow, requirements, options, assessments, resources, new courses, course reductions, integrating experiences, capstones).

Preparation

1. Post the First Generation Map (Gen 1 map) where it is visible to all.

2. Put a time limit on the meeting (1-2 hours).

3. Gather the group around the map, with an extra supply of Post-it® Notes (all four colors) and pencils for everyone.

4. Establish two rules:

   "All ideas are welcome."

   "Think like there is no box."

Focus the conversation around the map

1. Raise the initial interests and concerns that emerged in the first mapping session using the Emerging Issues List. Brainstorm options.

2. Focus specifically on the following:

- Identify where key assessments take place for each program outcome; add shadow Post-it® Notes that include the number of the program outcome. *See Figure 4: Alternative Energy Degree Program Map on pages 40–41.*
- Revisit the flow, finalizing the pencil lines and arrows with a fine point felt pen.
- Use Questions to Guide the Conversation for Second Generation Mapping (Figure 32, on page 86–87). Choose the questions that seem most critical to this program to begin the conversation. Others will emerge as the conversation goes deeper.

Assess the Program Map

1. Have the team use the Scoring Guide—Assessing the Quality of a Program Map (shown on page 89 or 141) to assess what they have done and to make any additions or changes that might be needed before showing it to others.

2. Have each team show their map; talk others through the flow.

3. In its large rough form, show your map to others (administrators, advisory groups, learners, etc.). Keeping it in a flexible (but fully legible) form makes everyone feel they can ask questions and potentially make a contribution.

Third Generation Program Mapping

Purpose

Third Generation Maps (Gen 3 maps) are digitally generated following graphic and color conventions. The purpose of Gen 3 mapping is to efficiently describe and communicate the program as an integrated learning experience, far more than a litany of courses or workshops, to the stakeholders and learners. While appearing "finished," a Gen 3 map will continue to both raise and answer questions, some of which will lead to future changes.

Prepare a digital file

1. Find someone on your staff that is willing and able to prepare the graphic file. While most of us can make a stab at using a simple word processing program, the best maps are created using specific graphic software. Decide on the quality you want and find the right person to do it. Sometimes the marketing, graphics or print departments will be able to do the job or suggest someone who might have the skills and interest to assist with the work. Or, ask someone to help you locate an open source piece of software that may be basic enough to allow many educators to create the maps using a simple template.

2. Be sure your map is legible and complete. This includes full course title and number on each course element, complete outcome statements, appropriate flow lines and arrows, and names of external partners.

3. Consider the use of color to provide contrast and distinction between the various elements of the maps. Depending upon complexity, color may be necessary to accurately

and logically show relationships and provide clarity. If the maps are to provide learners a program overview, serve as promotional pieces, have interactive capability, or present to in-house and community groups, color will most certainly need to be used.

Include maps on the web

1. Check with the appropriate person if you intend to place your map on a website. By planning ahead, you can make the map interactive and work with both web design and the graphics person to coordinate the efforts.

2. There are several workable open source pieces of software that can be used to create electronic versions of your map as it is being prepared for the web. Even using a simple Word template and saving it as a PDF might work for you.

3. A graphic designer should be able to assist with a template design and color selection. Here again, the web has a different set of standards than the print world and examples will need to be consulted for optimum rendering.

Make backup copies

1. Always keep backup copies of all your work whether it is in paper format or electronic, or both. Many hours of redundant work can be saved if backup copies are up-to-date and available.

2. When photographing your work, make certain you capture all the details of each element on the map (entry requirements, courses, capstone assessments, intended learning outcomes).

3. Secure all backup copies and make certain there is more than one copy, all located in places that are accessible as needed.

Best Practices for Facilitating Multiple Mapping Teams

As stated earlier, you can work with more than one group at a time to map their programs. In fact you can facilitate all your disciplines and programs in a multi-day event. This requires additional help and more preparation and planning. Here are some best practices we've identified over the decade when doing this work.

1. Select and prepare others to help you facilitate the process. Mapping a discipline or program is new for most instructors who will have lots of questions as the process gets started. Here is a way to get help:

   - Identify one person from each of the programs, bring them together an hour before the work session, and walk them through the process. They will be your assistant leaders in each team.
   - During the session, you will roam, assisting where and when needed. For a very large group, you will need a remote microphone and more assistants.

2. At the end of any multiple team session, have each team talk the other teams through their map—as the learner would experience it. This will be a highly valuable exercise for each of the teams.

Template: Emerging Issues List

Date: [   ]

Contributors:

[   ]

What needs further research, discussion, or decisions?	Who should be involved?	When will it be done?

Figure 36: Emerging Issues List

PART FIVE

Bringing It All Together in a Four-Page Curriculum Plan

We can hire instructors for their expertise in subject matter, but it is our responsibility to show them how their work (course) is connected to the larger picture of learner success.

Simplifying Curriculum Planning

As the use of web technology increases and education budgets shrink, organizations are using fewer and fewer full-time trainers and instructors. It is estimated that in community colleges nationwide, as many as 70% of the instructors are employed part-time, teaching courses that are handed to them as the need arises. This trend is also seen in universities as they attempt to reduce costs and long-term financial commitments.

While this is happening, colleges and training programs are finding it necessary to turn to professional instructional designers to construct programs and courses that can be delivered by a subject expert who may have little or no understanding of outcome-based learning strategies and assessment.

Where design professionals aren't used, organizations often fail to provide any significant assistance to instructors beyond suggesting a textbook and providing a copy of a syllabus that might be used. Under these circumstances, it is difficult to be accountable for learning outcomes, let alone understand the system for collecting and using learning data.

The answer is that colleges and workplace training programs must be prepared to provide instructors a clear plan for learning outcomes and assessment. This doesn't mean the organization dictates how they teach or train, but rather what learning outcomes are expected, what assessments should be conducted, and how the course aligns with and contributes to larger program and organization-wide learning outcomes. We think this kind of assistance can be given in four pages, so we call it the *Four-Page Curriculum Plan*.

We can hire for expertise in subject matter, but it is the organization's responsibility to help instructors see how their teaching assignments are connected to the larger picture of learner success, not only in their classrooms but in real-life roles. The organization must assume the responsibility to provide every full- and part-time instructor or trainer with no less than a *Four-Page Curriculum Plan*.

What is a *Four-Page Curriculum Plan*?

Unlike a syllabus or workshop handout that is written for the learner by the instructor, *Four-Page Curriculum Plans* are design documents for the instructor. It assures that all sections of a single course have continuity and focus on relevant learning outcomes. It is what every instructor deserves when asked to teach a course or conduct a workshop. It is something the organization provides in the interest of continuity and accountability for outcomes.

Here is what a Four-Page Curriculum Plan includes:

1. **Cover Page,** which introduces the instructor to the purpose of the *Four-Page Curriculum Plan,*

provides an overview of the components, describes how to use them, and defines terminology.

2. **Course Outcome Guide (COG),** which identifies the intended learning outcomes of one course within a program, its key assessment tasks and the essential content (concepts, issues, and skills) to be learned.

3. **Program Outcome Guide (POG),** if the course is an integral part of a program or training series. The POG shows the total scope of a program of studies including learning outcomes, key assessments, and essential content to which all courses must align.

4. **A current Program Map,** *showing the big picture,* how the course, as identified in the COG, is connected with other courses in the program, where the learners have been before, and where they expect to go afterwards.

None of these documents will tell instructors how to teach their courses. Instead, it will tell them:

- how to look at the course from a degree or program perspective;

- what the learners must be able to do in real life as a result of the course, in conjunction with a sequence of other courses; and

- what content the learners must master in the course to demonstrate the outcomes through specific assessment tasks.

On the following pages, review carefully the details of a *Four-Page Curriculum Plan*. You will find here an example gleaned from a college degree program in Alternative Energy, providing the meaningful concepts and terms used throughout this program, a Program Outcome Guide (POG), its Program Map, and one Course Outcome Guide (COG): AEP 212, Alternative Energy Systems. We think having a four-page plan of this kind would greatly assist any instructor, full- or part-time, to see not only how one's course fits into the big picture of a program but also in helping to plan and deliver such content to learners.

A very important note: To develop a COG or POG, go to the following two primers in this series: *The OUTCOME Primer: Envisioning Learning Outcomes,* and *The CONTENT Primer: Aligning Essential Content with Learning Outcomes.*

Examples of the Four-Page Curriculum Plan

Four-Page Curriculum Plan for the Alternative Energy Degree Program

Along with this introductory page, you are being provided with three important design documents that will guide you in the development and delivery of the course you teach. This course was designed using an outcomes-based framework that uses a backwards design process. See the descriptions below. The course you teach is part of a learning system that was designed to meet specific learning outcomes at the course, program, and organization-wide level.

The first document, the Course Outcome Guide (COG), provides the learning outcomes that all learners should be able to do by the completion of the course. The second document, the Program Outcome Guide (POG), provides the learning outcomes that all learners should be able to do by the completion of the program. Both design documents provide the essential concepts, skills and issues to be applied and the key assessment tasks that will best provide evidence of learners' mastery of the learning outcomes at the course and program level. The final document, the Program Map is a visual representation of the learner's journey through the program. You can clearly see where the course you teach fits into the overall program including any prerequisite course(s) and the connections with other courses.

Use these design documents as you develop any learning activities, discussions, assignments, to ensure that they include the concepts, skills, issues and assessments in order to meet all the outcomes. You may be asked to submit samples of learner's work (i.e. artifacts) so that it can be included in the college's assessment process that provides evidence of learning and areas for improvement.

Here are definitions for some of the terms we use in this curriculum plan:

Term	Meaning
Academic program	A highly organized set of experiences learners navigate through that usually culminates in a specific degree or certificate.
Assessment	Ongoing process aimed at understanding and improving learning by systematically gathering, analyzing, and interpreting evidence of intended learning outcomes.
Assessment tasks	Complex and significant tasks learners complete to demonstrate the intended learning outcome (e.g. projects, portfolios, presentations, problem solutions, demonstrations, simulations, role-plays) . Often referred to as performance tasks.
Backwards design	A process of beginning with an intended learning outcome, then working backwards to determine appropriate assessment tasks and essential content (concepts to be applied, issues to be solved and skills to be mastered); a process used at the organization, program and course level.
Concepts	Ideas that learners must understand in order to achieve the intended learning outcome; emphasis on depth of understanding rather than breadth of information.
Course Outcome Guide (COG)	A one-page plan focusing on intended course learning outcomes and working backwards to determine essential course content. (Also known as WOG or SOG when used for workshops or sessions.)
Issues	Problems and challenges that learners must be able to resolve in order to achieve the intended learning outcomes.
Learning outcomes	Statements that describe a vision of what learners will be able to do outside the classroom (in real-life roles) as the result of their learning. Learning outcomes are short, concise and detailed descriptions that provide the road map for guiding course, program, and organizational level learning.
Outcome-based framework	A curriculum design approach which begins with a vision of what we hope learners will be able to DO outside and beyond the classroom, in real-life roles, with what they learn in a program, course, or workshop/training.
Program Outcome Guide (POG)	A one-page plan focusing on intended program learning outcomes and working backwards to determine essential content for a program.
Real-life roles	The roles that learners take on in their personal and/or work lives, such as family member, life-long learner, supervisor, medical assistant, etc.
Skills	Abilities that are essential to the learning outcome, usually learned and mastered through practice and feedback. Combined with what the learner must understand (concepts and issues), these form the content of the learning experience.

Figure 37: Four-Page Curriculum Plan for the Alternative Energy Degree Program (page 1 of 4)

POG/COG/WOG TITLE: COG: AEP 212-Alternative Energy Systems   **Date:** _____

Concepts & Issues

What must the learners understand to demonstrate the intended outcome?

-Energy sources
-Solar
-Wind
-Fuel cells
-Fossil fuels
-Reactions
-Power
-Consumption
-Energy quantification
-Convection current
-Kinetic energy
-Evaluation models
-Site Assessments

-Safety (self, community, environment)
-Feasibility (technical, economic, environmental)
-Return on Investment

What issues must the learners be able to resolve to demonstrate the outcome?

Skills

What skills must the learners master to demonstrate the intended outcome?

1. Argue the pros and cons of energy systems.
2. Classify alternative energy resources.
3. Analyze facts and statistical data.
4. Fabricate and test prototypes.
5. Use science principles of electronics, chemistry, physics, mechanics.
6. Work safely and use personal protection equipment.
7. Contribute responsibly to the efforts of a team.
8. Use logic and reasoning to support decisions.
9. Accept feedback on design projects.
10. Make adjustments in thinking based on feedback from supervisors.

Assessment Tasks

What will learners do in here to demonstrate evidence of the outcome?

1. Choose an alternative energy system. Write a position paper and speak to the class for 15 minutes on the pros and cons of that system.
2. In teams, design and build three simple energy system prototypes: solar, wind, and fuel cell.
3. Conduct an energy site assessment and propose an alternative energy solution that includes current system identification, benefits of proposed system, costs (materials and labor), and timeline.

Intended Outcomes

What do learners need to be able to DO "out there" in the rest of life that we're responsible for "in here"?

1. Investigate the technical, economical, and environmental potential and progress of new and emerging forms of power generation.
2. Use the principles of science (electricity, mechanics, chemistry, physics, mathematics) to fabricate and test energy prototypes.
3. Follow industry quality and safety procedures in the use of personal gear, equipment and tools.

Figure 37: Four-Page Curriculum Plan—Alternative Energy Degree Program (page 2 of 4)

POG/COG/WOG TITLE: POG: Alternative Energy Degree Program

Date: _____

Concepts & Issues	Skills	Assessment Tasks	Intended Outcomes
What must the learners understand to demonstrate the intended outcome?	*What skills must the learners master to demonstrate the intended outcome?*	*What will learners do in here to demonstrate evidence of the outcome?*	*What do learners need to be able to DO "out there" in the rest of life that we're responsible for "in here"?*
-Energy sources: solar, wind, fuel cells -Fossil fuels -Heat transfer -Chemical reaction -Power systems -Energy consumption -Photovoltaic systems -Hydro-electricity -Energy quantification -Electrolysis -PEM (proton exchange membrane) -Convection current -Kinetic energy -Evaluation models -Site Assessments -Safety (self, community, environment) -Feasibility of systems -Return on Investment	1. Argue for the pros and cons of alternative energy. 2. Classify alternative energy resources by use, availability, and environmental impact. 3. Analyze energy systems according to efficiency, economics, and environment. 4. Design, fabricate and test prototypes. 5. Apply science principles of electronics, chemistry, physics, mechanics to design and test systems. 6. Conduct laboratory experiments. 7. Work safely and use personal protection equipment. 8. Contribute responsibly to the efforts of a team. 9. Evaluate energy systems.	1. Write position papers and make presentations on the pros and cons of at least three alternative energy systems: wind, solar, and fuel cells. 2. Assess renewable energy resources for residential and commercial customers in wind, solar, and fuel cells. 3. Individually conduct a site assessment with specific recommendations based on data. 4. Design residential and commercial energy systems in wind, solar, and fuel cells based on a comprehensive assessment and customer requirements. 5. Install, maintain, and troubleshoot alternative energy systems.	1. Demonstrate effective verbal and written communication skills as an individual and team member. 2. Demonstrate basic electrical, mechanical, chemical, mathematical and computer skills involved in maintaining alternative energy systems. 3. Apply sound business and economic principles to achieve and maintain profitability of alternative energy systems. 4. Follow quality and safety procedures. 5. Install, repair, & design alternative energy systems. 6. Fabricate and test prototypes. 7. Participate in researching current and emerging alternative energy systems.

What issues must the learners be able to resolve to demonstrate the outcome?

Figure 37: Four-Page Curriculum Plan—Alternative Energy Degree Program (page 3 of 4)

Alternative Energy Degree Program Map

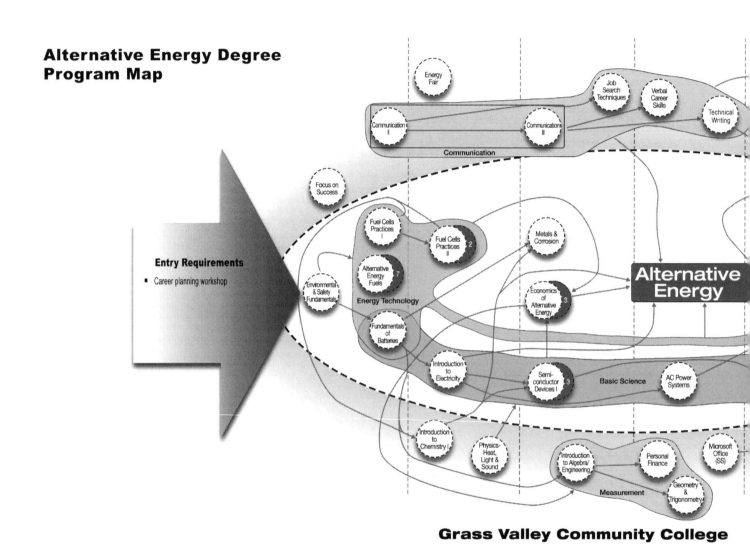

Figure 37: Four-Page Curriculum Plan—Alternative Energy Degree Program (page 4 of 4)

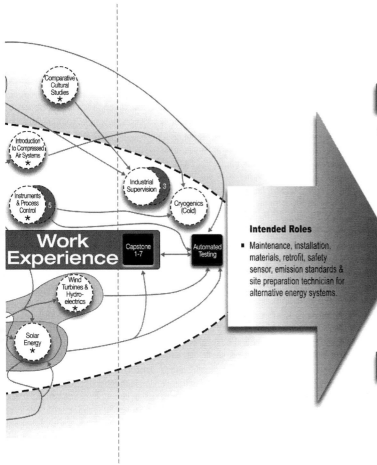

★ Courses in the Bahamas

INTENDED LEARNING OUTCOMES

1. Demonstrate effective verbal and written communication skills as an individual and as a team member.

2. Demonstrate basic electrical, mechanical, chemical, mathematical and computer skills involved in maintaining alternative energy systems.

3. Apply sound business and economic principles to achieve and maintain profitability of alternative energy systems.

4. Follow quality and safety procedures.

5. Install, repair and design alternative energy systems.

6. Fabricate and test prototypes.

7. Participate in researching current and emerging alternative energy systems.

ORGANIZATION-WIDE LEARNING OUTCOMES

- Communicate effectively
- Think critically
- Practice from a code of ethics
- Interact well with others
- Show evidence of cultural and global awareness

Four-Page Curriculum Plan for the Executive Leadership Program

Along with this introductory page, you are being provided with three important design documents that will guide you in the development and delivery of the course you teach. This course was designed using an outcomes-based framework that uses a backwards design process. See the descriptions below. The course you teach is part of a learning system that was designed to meet specific learning outcomes at the course, program, and organization-wide level.

The first document, the Course Outcome Guide (COG), provides the learning outcomes that all learners should be able to do by the completion of the course. The second document, the Program Outcome Guide (POG), provides the learning outcomes that all learners should be able to do by the completion of the program. Both design documents provide the essential concepts, skills and issues to be applied and the key assessment tasks that will best provide evidence of learners' mastery of the learning outcomes at the course and program level. The final document, the Program Map is a visual representation of the learner's journey through the program. You can clearly see where the course you teach fits into the overall program including any prerequisite course(s) and the connections with other courses.

Use these design documents as you develop any learning activities, discussions, assignments, to ensure that they include the concepts, skills, issues and assessments in order to meet all the outcomes. You may be asked to submit samples of learner's work (i.e. artifacts) so that it can be included in the college's assessment process that provides evidence of learning and areas for improvement.

Here are definitions for some of the terms we use in this curriculum plan:

Term	Meaning
Academic program	A highly organized set of experiences learners navigate through that usually culminates in a specific degree or certificate.
Assessment	Ongoing process aimed at understanding and improving learning by systematically gathering, analyzing, and interpreting evidence of intended learning outcomes.
Assessment tasks	Complex and significant tasks learners complete to demonstrate the intended learning outcome (e.g. projects, portfolios, presentations, problem solutions, demonstrations, simulations, role-plays) . Often referred to as performance tasks.
Backwards design	A process of beginning with an intended learning outcome, then working backwards to determine appropriate assessment tasks and essential content (concepts to be applied, issues to be solved and skills to be mastered); a process used at the organization, program and course level.
Concepts	Ideas that learners must understand in order to achieve the intended learning outcome; emphasis on depth of understanding rather than breadth of information.
Course Outcome Guide (COG)	A one-page plan focusing on intended course learning outcomes and working backwards to determine essential course content. (Also known as WOG or SOG when used for workshops or sessions.)
Issues	Problems and challenges that learners must be able to resolve in order to achieve the intended learning outcomes.
Learning outcomes	Statements that describe a vision of what learners will be able to do outside the classroom (in real-life roles) as the result of their learning. Learning outcomes are short, concise and detailed descriptions that provide the road map for guiding course, program, and organizational level learning.
Outcome-based framework	A curriculum design approach which begins with a vision of what we hope the learner will be able to DO outside and beyond the classroom, in real-life roles, with what he/she learns in a program, course, or workshop/training.
Program Outcome Guide (POG)	A one-page plan focusing on intended program learning outcomes and working backwards to determine essential content for a program.
Real-life roles	The roles that learners take on in their personal and/or work lives, such as family member, life-long learner, supervisor, medical assistant, etc.
Skills	Abilities that are essential to the learning outcome, usually learned and mastered through practice and feedback. Combined with what the learner must understand (concepts and issues), these form the content of the learning experience.

Figure 38: Four-Page Curriculum Plan—Executive Leadership (page 1 of 4)

POG/COG/WOG TITLE: _____ WOG: Strategic Planning Workshop _____   **Date:** _____

Concepts & Issues	Skills	Assessment Tasks	Intended Outcomes
What must the learners understand to demonstrate the intended outcome?	*What skills must the learners master to demonstrate the intended outcome?*	*What will learners do in here to demonstrate evidence of the outcome?*	*What do learners need to be able to DO "out there" in the rest of life that we're responsible for "in here"?*
• Strategies vs tactics • Strategic planning • Strategic inquiry • Strategic thinking • Operational planning • Decision making • Execution • Human Capital and resources • Measurement • Organizational outcomes • Monitoring and adjusting	1. Evaluate a strategic plan. 2. Determine human capital needs.	1. Evaluate a current strategic plan, determine and make changes needed, given a change in organizational priorities. 2. Present an updated strategic plan highlighting organizational alignment.	1. Determine strategies, align organizational priorities and human capital needs in order to execute, measure and meet organizational outcomes.
• Competing priorities • Changing conditions • Uncertainty			

What issues must the learners be able to resolve to demonstrate the outcome?

Figure 38: Four-Page Curriculum Plan—Executive Leadership (page 2 of 4)

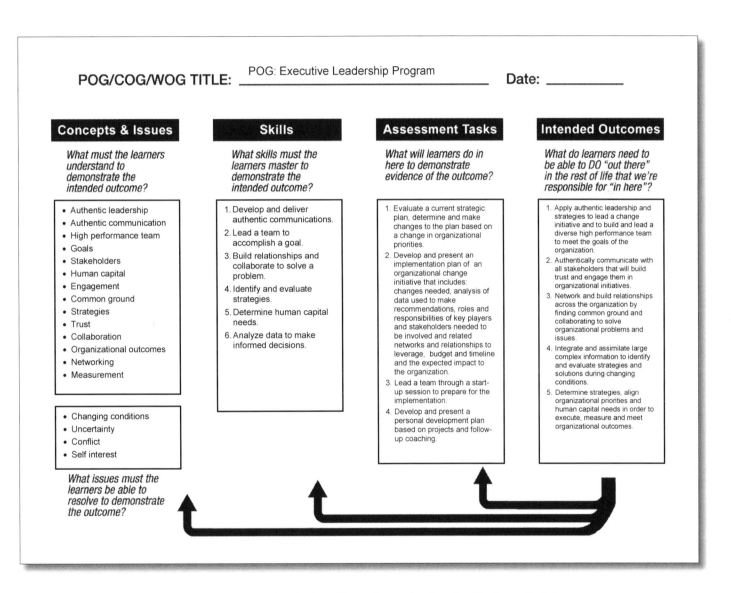

POG/COG/WOG TITLE: POG: Executive Leadership Program   **Date:** _____

Concepts & Issues	**Skills**	**Assessment Tasks**	**Intended Outcomes**
What must the learners understand to demonstrate the intended outcome?	*What skills must the learners master to demonstrate the intended outcome?*	*What will learners do in here to demonstrate evidence of the outcome?*	*What do learners need to be able to DO "out there" in the rest of life that we're responsible for "in here"?*

Concepts & Issues:
- Authentic leadership
- Authentic communication
- High performance team
- Goals
- Stakeholders
- Human capital
- Engagement
- Common ground
- Strategies
- Trust
- Collaboration
- Organizational outcomes
- Networking
- Measurement

- Changing conditions
- Uncertainty
- Conflict
- Self interest

What issues must the learners be able to resolve to demonstrate the outcome?

Skills:
1. Develop and deliver authentic communications.
2. Lead a team to accomplish a goal.
3. Build relationships and collaborate to solve a problem.
4. Identify and evaluate strategies.
5. Determine human capital needs.
6. Analyze data to make informed decisions.

Assessment Tasks:
1. Evaluate a current strategic plan, determine and make changes to the plan based on a change in organizational priorities.
2. Develop and present an implementation plan of an organizational change initiative that includes: changes needed, analysis of data used to make recommendations, roles and responsibilities of key players and stakeholders needed to be involved and related networks and relationships to leverage, budget and timeline and the expected impact to the organization.
3. Lead a team through a start-up session to prepare for the implementation.
4. Develop and present a personal development plan based on projects and follow-up coaching.

Intended Outcomes:
1. Apply authentic leadership and strategies to lead a change initiative and to build and lead a diverse high performance team to meet the goals of the organization.
2. Authentically communicate with all stakeholders that will build trust and engage them in organizational initiatives.
3. Network and build relationships across the organization by finding common ground and collaborating to solve organizational problems and issues.
4. Integrate and assimilate large complex information to identify and evaluate strategies and solutions during changing conditions.
5. Determine strategies, align organizational priorities and human capital needs in order to execute, measure and meet organizational outcomes.

Figure 38: Four-PageCurriculum Plan—Executive Leadership (page 3 of 4)

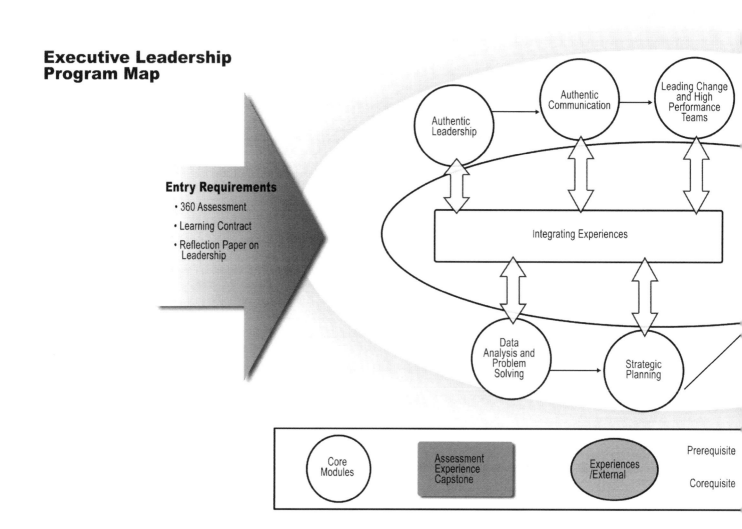

Figure 38: Curriculum Plan—Executive Leadership (page 4 of 4)

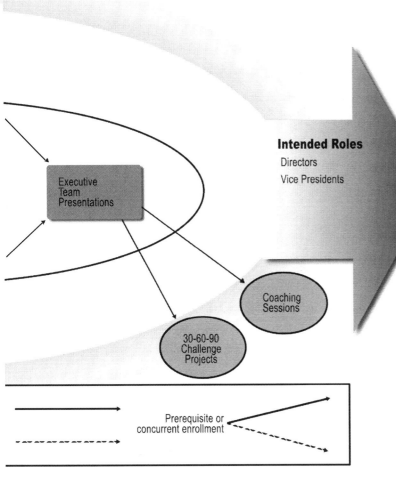

Intended Roles

Directors

Vice Presidents

INTENDED LEARNING OUTCOMES

- Applies authentic leadership and strategies to lead a change initative and to build and lead a diverse high performance team to meet the goals of the organization.

  - Authentically communicates with all stakeholders that will build trust and engage them in organizational initiatives.

    - Networks and builds relationships across the organization by finding common ground and collaborating to solve organizational problems and issues.

  - Integrates and assimilates large complex information to identify and evaluate strategies and solutions during changing conditions.

- Determines strategies, aligns organizational priorities and human capital needs in order to execute, measure and meet organizational outcomes.

Executive Team Presentations

Coaching Sessions

30-60-90 Challenge Projects

Prerequisite or concurrent enrollment

PART SIX
Continuing Your Learning

In Conclusion

In this *MAPPING Primer: Mapping the Way to Learning Outcomes*, we have focused our discussion on the process of mapping a learner's journey through workplace training and college programs. As noted at the beginning of this book, here is what we envisioned that you would be able to do after working carefully through this Primer:

- **Create a visual map of the learner's journey through a series of learning experiences in programs and courses.**
- **Facilitate mapping sessions to align outcomes, improve sequencing, and use resources to achieve intended learning outcomes.**

Next Steps

Each of the other books in *The Outcome Primers Series 2.0* is designed to build your capacity to do specific things that relate to curricular mapping. The intended learning outcomes for each of the Primers in this series are stated here.

The OUTCOME Primer: Envisioning Learning Outcomes, Stiehl and Sours

Working through this book should help build your capacity to:

Envision and develop concise and robust learning outcome statements that are relevant to life roles and drive essential content and assessment in training and educational programs; help others understand learning outcomes as essential for effective instruction.

The ASSESSMENT Primer: Assessing and Tracking Evidence of Learning Outcomes, Stiehl and Null

Working through this book should help build your capacity to:

Develop tasks, tools and systemic processes for assessing and tracking evidence of learning outcomes to assist and advance learners and

continuously improve learning experiences (at the course, program and organization levels).

The CONTENT Primer: Aligning Content with Learning Outcomes, Stiehl and Decker

Working through this book should help build your capacity to:

Work to identify, delimit, and align essential content with learning outcomes by designing backwards, outside in; design programs, courses, and workshops from a contemporary, constructivist understanding of learning.

The GUIDING Primer: Guiding Learners Toward Intended Outcomes, Prickel and Stiehl

Working through this book should help build your capacity to:

Move beyond the old-school perception of what it means to *teach* to *guiding* learners in the pursuit of intended learning outcomes.

The SUSTAINABILITY Primer: Sustaining Learning Outcomes and Assessment, Telban and Stiehl

Working through this book should help build your capacity to:

Create and sustain an outcomes and assessment system through effective leadership, instructor involvement, professional development, and system integration.

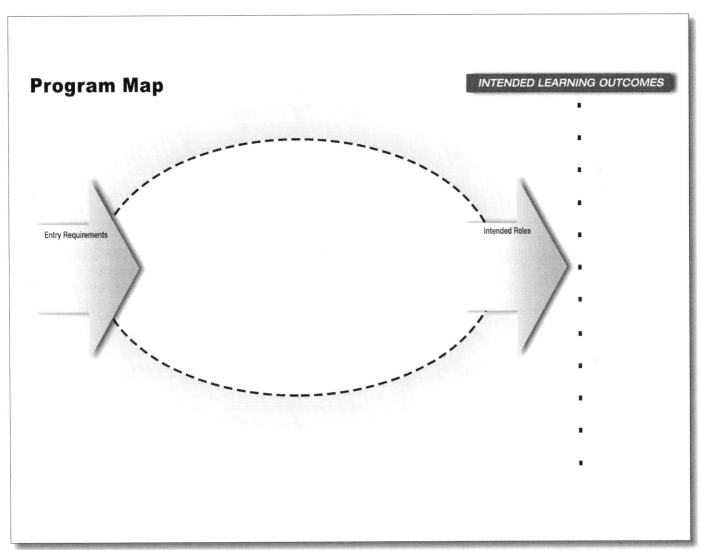

Program Map

INTENDED LEARNING OUTCOMES

Entry Requirements

Intended Roles

Program Map

Template: Course Activity Map	Course: _____		Term: _____			
	Week 1–3	**Week 4–6**	**Week 7–9**	**Week 10–13**	**Week 14–16**	**Week 17**
Develop a deep understanding of these major concepts						
Face these issues						
Master these skills						
Show Learning Proficiency (Key Assessments)						

Course Activity Map

Template: Four-Page Curriculum Plan for _____ (course or workshop)

Along with this introductory page, you are being provided with three important design documents that will guide you in the development and delivery of the course you teach. This course was designed using an outcomes-based framework that uses a backwards design process. See the descriptions below. The course you teach is part of a learning system that was designed to meet specific learning outcomes at the course, program, and organization-wide level.

The first document, the Course Outcome Guide (COG), provides the learning outcomes that all learners should be able to do by the completion of the course. The second document, the Program Outcome Guide (POG), provides the learning outcomes that all learners should be able to do by the completion of the program. Both design documents provide the essential concepts, skills and issues to be applied and the key assessment tasks that will best provide evidence of learners' mastery of the learning outcomes at the course and program level. The final document, the Program Map is a visual representation of the learner's journey through the program. You can clearly see where the course you teach fits into the overall program including any prerequisite course(s) and the connections with other courses.

Use these design documents as you develop any learning activities, discussions, assignments, to ensure that they include the concepts, skills, issues and assessments in order to meet all the outcomes. You may be asked to submit samples of learner's work (i.e. artifacts) so that it can be included in the college's assessment process that provides evidence of learning and areas for improvement.

Here are definitions for some of the terms we use in this curriculum plan:

Term	Meaning
Academic program	A highly organized set of experiences learners navigate through that usually culminates in a specific degree or certificate.
Assessment	Ongoing process aimed at understanding and improving learning by systematically gathering, analyzing, and interpreting evidence of intended learning outcomes.
Assessment tasks	Complex and significant tasks learners complete to demonstrate the intended learning outcome (e.g. projects, portfolios, presentations, problem solutions, demonstrations, simulations, role-plays) . Often referred to as performance tasks.
Backwards design	A process of beginning with an intended learning outcome, then working backwards to determine appropriate assessment tasks and essential content (concepts to be applied, issues to be solved and skills to be mastered); a process used at the organization, program and course level.
Concepts	Ideas that learners must understand in order to achieve the intended learning outcome; emphasis on depth of understanding rather than breadth of information.
Course Outcome Guide (COG)	A one-page plan focusing on intended course learning outcomes and working backwards to determine essential course content. (Also known as WOG or SOG when used for workshops or sessions.)
Issues	Problems and challenges that learners must be able to resolve in order to achieve the intended learning outcomes.
Learning outcomes	Statements that describe a vision of what learners will be able to do outside the classroom (in real-life roles) as the result of their learning. Learning outcomes are short, concise and detailed descriptions that provide the road map for guiding course, program, and organizational level learning.
Outcomes-based framework	A curriculum design approach which begins with a vision of what we hope the learner will be able to DO outside and beyond the classroom, in real-life roles, with what he/she learns in a program, course, or workshop/training.
Program Outcome Guide (POG)	A one-page plan focusing on intended program learning outcomes and working backwards to determine essential content for a program.
Real-life roles	The roles that learners take on in their personal and/or work lives, such as family member, life-long learner, supervisor, medical assistant, etc.
Skills	Abilities that are essential to the learning outcome, usually learned and mastered through practice and feedback. Combined with what the learner must understand (concepts and issues), these form the content of the learning experience.

Four-Page Curriculum Plan (page 1 of 4)

POG/COG/WOG TITLE: __COG:_____ Date: _____

Concepts & Issues

What must the learners understand to demonstrate the intended outcome?

Skills

What skills must the learners master to demonstrate the intended outcome?

Assessment Tasks

What will learners do in here to demonstrate evidence of the outcome?

Intended Outcomes

What do learners need to be able to DO "out there" in the rest of life that we're responsible for "in here"?

What issues must the learners be able to resolve to demonstrate the outcome?

Four-Page Curriculum Plan (page 2 of 4)

POG/COG/WOG TITLE: _____ **POG:** _____ **Date:** _____

Concepts & Issues	Skills	Assessment Tasks	Intended Outcomes
What must the learners understand to demonstrate the intended outcome?	*What skills must the learners master to demonstrate the intended outcome?*	*What will learners do in here to demonstrate evidence of the outcome?*	*What do learners need to be able to DO "out there" in the rest of life that we're responsible for "in here"?*

What issues must the learners be able to resolve to demonstrate the outcome?

Four-Page Curriculum Plan (page 3 of 4)

Program Map

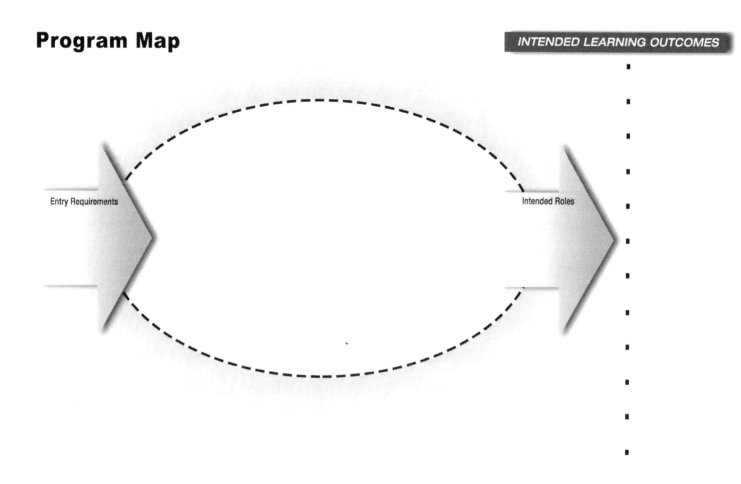

Four-Page Curriculum Plan (page 4 of 4)

Template: Scoring Guide—Assessing the Quality of a Program Map

Characteristics of Good Program Maps				Suggestions for Improvement
Rating scale: 1=absent 2=present				
1. Use of Conventions	1	2		
Map includes the following basic descriptions: • Program name • Organization name/logo • Date • Entry requirements • Intended roles • Intended learning outcomes (program or organization-wide) Separate colors are used to distinguish types of courses (learning experiences) according to the map legend.				
Rating scale: 1=absent 2=present 3=changes needed				
2. Learning Experiences	1	2	3	
Where learning experiences (courses) are placed on the map reveals where they are offered in relation to the whole organization.				
3. Interdependencies	1	2	3	
The map clearly illustrates how courses interrelate (whether linear or nonlinear). These relationships are expressed through tight sequences, theme clusters, and directional arrows.				
4. Integration of Learning	1	2	3	
Careful consideration has been given to appropriately illustrate any integrative learning experience.				
5. Capstone Assessment	1	2	3	
It is clear where each program learning outcome and organization-wide learning outcome is being assessed.				

Our Preferred Terms for Curricular Mapping

Term	Meaning
Academic program	A highly organized set of experiences learners navigate through that usually culminates in a specific degree or certificate.
Assessment	Ongoing process aimed at understanding and improving learning for systematically gathering, analyzing and interpreting evidence of intended learning outcomes.
Assessment tasks	Complex and significant tasks learners complete to demonstrate the intended outcome (e.g. projects, portfolios, presentations, problem solutions, demonstrations, simulations, role-plays); often referred to as performance tasks.
Backwards design	A process of beginning with an intended outcome, then working backwards to determine appropriate assessment tasks and essential content (concepts to be learned, issues to be solved and skills to be mastered); a process used at the organization, program and course level.
Capstone assessment tasks	A piece of work, e.g., presentation, project, problem-solution, procedure, e-portfolio, poster session, proposal, paper, that provides evidence of the intended outcome at culminating point(s) in the program; can be distributed across the program and/or concentrated at the end.
Concepts	Ideas that learners must understand in order to achieve the intended outcome; emphasis on depth of understanding rather than breadth of information.
Course Outcome Guide (COG)	A tool for collaboratively developing a one-page plan focusing on a course's intended learning outcomes and working backwards to determine essential course content. Also known as a WOG or SOG when used for workshops or sessions.
Guide's *guide*	A term used to describe the essential role that learning outcomes play in guiding learners.
Issues	Problems and challenges that learners must be able to resolve in order to achieve the intended outcomes.

Our Preferred Terms for Curricular Mapping

Term	Meaning
Learner's journey	A flow of learning events that learners navigate through to achieve the intended learning outcomes.
Learning outcomes	Statements that describe a vision of what learners will be able to do outside the classroom (in real-life roles) as the result of their learning. Learning outcomes are short, concise and detailed descriptions that provide the road map for guiding course, program, and organizational level learning.
Outcome-based framework	A curriculum design approach which begins with a vision of what we hope the learner will be able to DO outside and beyond the classroom, in real-life roles, with what he/she learns in a program, course, or workshop/training.
Outside-in design	Curriculum design process that begins by envisioning what the learners need to be able to do "out there" (outside the classroom) in the rest of life.
Program	A highly organized set of learning experiences that learners navigate and result in intended learning outcomes, with some leading to a certificate or licensure.
Program Map	The organization and visual depiction of the learner's journey through learning experiences and assessments aligned to achieve intended learning outcomes; a systemic view of planned learning experiences—entrance to exit..
Program Outcome Guide (POG)	A one-page plan focusing on intended program learning outcomes and working backwards to determine essential content for a program.
Real-life roles	The roles that learners take on in their personal and/or work lives, such as *family member, life-long learner, supervisor, medical assistant, etc.*
Scoring guide	A qualitative assessment tool that explicitly describes the standards for good performance to help the learner know what "good" looks like; can be used by learners, evaluators, or assessors to provide feedback to improve performance or product.
Skills	Abilities that are essential to the outcome, usually learned and mastered through practice and feedback. Combined with what the learner must understand (concepts and issues), these form the content of the learning experience.

What we wanted to do in this bibliography was to give a sense of the breadth of writings that have influenced this work. While some support for these models come from educational literature, much more comes from the literature of science and organizational development. All of these works have helped us think more systemically about teaching and learning in the context of a "greening" society.

Visual Design and Visual Tools

Nisbett, Richard. (2003). *The geography of thought: How Asians and Westerners think differently ... and why*. New York: Simon & Schuster.

Volk, Tyler. (1995). *Metapatterns: Across space, time and mind*. New York: Columbia University Press.

Systems Thinking

Benyus. Janine M. (1997). *Biomimicry*. New York: Harper Collins.

Capra, Fritjof. (2002). *The hidden connections: Integrating the biological, cognitive, and social dimensions of life into a science of sustainability*. New York: Doubleday.

Capra, Fritjof. (1996). *The web of life: A new scientific understanding of living systems*. New York: Doubleday.

Meadows. Donella H. (2008). *Thinking in Systems*. Vermont: Chelsea Green.

Locke, John L. (1999). *Why we don't talk to each other anymore: The de-voicing of society*. New York: Simon & Schuster.

Pink, Daniel. (2006). *A whole new mind: Why right-brainers will rule the future*. New York: Penguin Group.

Sanders. T. Irene. (1998). *Strategic thinking and the new science*. New York: Simon and Schuster.

Wheatley. Margaret J. (2002). *Turning to one another: Simple conversations to restore hope to the future*. New York: Simon & Schuster.

Wheatley, Margaret & Kellner-Rogers, Myron. (1996). *A simpler way*. San Francisco: Berrett-Koehler.

College Curriculum Development

Allen, M. with Sites, R. (2012). *Leaving ADDIE for SAM: An agile model for developing the best learning experiences*. Alexandria, Virginia: American Society for Training and Development (ASTD) Press.

Bloom, B. S., Engelhart, N. D., Furst, E. J. et al. (1956). *Taxonomy of educational objectives: The classification of educational goals. Handbook 1: cognitive domain*. New York: David McKay Company.

Caine, Renate N. & Caine, Geoffrey. (1994). *Making connections: Teaching and the human brain*. New York: Addison-Wesley.

Costa, Arthur L. & Liebmann, Rosemarie. (1997). *Envisioning process as content: Toward a renaissance curriculum*. Thousand Oaks, CA: Corwin Press.

Prickel, Don & Stiehl, Ruth. (2012). *Watermarks: A Guiding Primer for Part- & Full-time College Faculty*. USA: Create Space.

Stiehl, Ruth & Lewchuk, Les. (2008). *The ASSESSMENT Primer: Creating a flow of learning evidence*. Corvallis, Oregon: The Learning Organization.

Stiehl, Ruth & Lewchuk, Les. (2008). *The OUTCOMES Primer: Reconstructing the college curriculum* (3rd ed.) Corvallis, Oregon: The Learning Organization.

Stiehl, Ruth & Lewchuk, Les. (2012). *The MAPPING Primer: Tools for Reconstructing the College Curriculum* (2nd ed.) Corvallis, Oregon: The Learning Organization.

Acknowledgments

Our thanks go to the hundreds of individuals in colleges, agencies and industry who, through our teaching and consulting experiences with them, have helped to shape our understanding of learning outcomes and assessment over the years. Without these experiences, we would have had nothing at all to say.

As just one part of a six-part series, this Primer wasn't created by us alone. We are deeply indebted to our full team on *The OUTCOME Primers Series 2.0*: Don Prickel, Lori Sours, Lynn Null, Michele Decker, Geoffrey Floyd and Robin McBride. This team has never failed to inspire us. They have each demonstrated a high level of intellectual honesty concerning our work and have paddled the rapids with us on the way to the *take-out*.

Additional credit goes to the educators and administrators at Cuyahoga Community College for engaging with us in this work and being committed to outcome-based education. We had many opportunities to work together and implement many of the concepts and ideas expressed in this work. We are glad you invited us into your raft.

—Kathy Telban
Ruth Stiehl
2017

Ruth E. Stiehl, Ed.D.
PROFESSOR EMERITUS, INSTRUCTIONAL SYSTEMS, OREGON STATE UNIVERSITY
CO-FOUNDER, WHITE WATER INSTITUTE FOR LEADERSHIP TRAINING
FOUNDER, THE LEARNING ORGANIZATION

Dr. Stiehl, a thought leader on learning outcomes assessment for over twenty years, was lead author on the acclaimed original series of *THE OUTCOME PRIMERS*. Over a period of fifteen years this original series guided colleges across the United States and Canada as they prepared for new accreditation standards for outcomes assessment. Along with a team of new co-authors and consultants at The Learning Organization, she has expanded the work beyond colleges to workplace training, including agencies, business and industry. In contrast to the work of many academics, all of the writing, speaking and workshops produced by The Learning Organization are charged with story, metaphor, and integrated learning. Dr. Stiehl lives and works in Corvallis, Oregon.

Kathy Telban, CPT, SPHR, M.Ed.
PRESIDENT, CHIEF OUTCOME STRATEGIST AND COACH, iSOLVit LLC
PAST BOARD MEMBER, WHITE WATER INSTITUTE FOR LEADERSHIP TRAINING
FORMER DIRECTOR OF CURRICULUM DEVELOPMENT AND LEARNING OUTCOME ASSESSMENT, CUYAHOGA COMMUNITY COLLEGE

Kathy Telban is a multi-dimensional professional with over 20 years of industry experience in information technology, technical training, sales, human resource, workforce development and organizational effectiveness. She has spent the last decade in higher education designing, implementing and improving outcome-based education and assessment processes. In addition to holding in-house administrative positions, she has coached college faculty and administrators in systems planning across the US and Canada. Kathy is particularly passionate about helping organizations improve their outcomes where everyone matters, which is the key tenet of her company, iSOLVit. Kathy lives in Cleveland, Ohio and can be reached through *www.isolvit.org* and/or *www.outcomeprimers.com*.

Authors can be contacted at *strategists@outcomeprimers.com*.

Don Prickel, Ph.D.
EXECUTIVE EDITOR

Dr. Prickel, one of the lead authors in the Outcome Primers Series 2.0, has also served in the major role of executive editor for all six primers, assuring continuity within the series. He brings to this work many years of experience as an adult educator and consultant to colleges and universities on instructional strategies and adult learning theory.

The authors of *The OUTCOME Primers Series 2.0* are available to consult in person with you and your organization in the following ways:

- Facilitating work sessions in outcomes and assessment planning at any level of the organization
- Face-to-face and on-line coaching, advising, and providing counsel to leaders, committees, and instructors on outcomes and assessment

Contact us through our website:
www.outcomeprimers.com
or
email us at: *strategists@outcomeprimers.com*